D0895666

WORKING WORDS IN

Spelling

G. Willard Woodruff and George N. Moore

with Robert G. Forest, Richard A. Talbot, Ann R. Talbot

G

GREAT SOURCE EDUCATION GROUP

A Houghton Mifflin Company

Wilmington, Massachusetts

Contents

Art and design credits appear on page 192.

Copyright © 1998 by D.C. Heath and Company, a division of Houghton Mifflin Company

All rights reserved. No part of this work may be reproduced or transmitted in any form by any means, electronic or mechanical, including photocopying, recording, or any information storage or retrieval system, without the prior written permission of Great Source Education Group, Inc., unless such copying is expressly permitted by federal copyright law. Address inquiries to Permissions, Great Source Education Group, Inc., 181 Ballardvale Street, Wilmington, MA 01887.

Handwriting models in this book are reproduced with permission of Zaner-Bloser, Inc., © 1990.

Printed in the United States of America

Great Source is a trademark of Houghton Mifflin Company.

International Standard Book Number: 0-669-45947-X

2 3 4 5 6 7 8 9 10 - VHP - 04 03 02

Become a
SHARP speller

See the word.

- Look at the word.
- Think about the letters that spell the word.

Hear the word.

- Say the word.
- Listen to the consonant and vowel sounds.

Adopt the word.

- Close your eyes.
- See the word in your mind's eye.
- Think how it looks and sounds.

Record the word.

- Cover the word.
- Write the word.

Proofread the word.

- Correct the word.
- Touch each letter.
- Think about the word again.

1

A. Pretest and Proofreading

B. Spelling Words and Phrases

1. failure	success or <u>failure</u>	
2. frail	<u>frail</u> and delicate	
3. prevail	cannot <u>prevail</u> against	
4. available	no longer <u>available</u>	
5. praising	<u>praising</u> their performance	
6. await	to <u>await</u> their arrival	
7. regain	may <u>regain</u> consciousness	
8. container	<u>container</u> of milk	
9. entertainment	musical <u>entertainment</u>	
10. acquaint	will <u>acquaint</u> us	
11. acquaintance	just an <u>acquaintance</u>	
12. campaign	presidential <u>campaign</u>	
13. affair	<u>affair</u> of state	
14. despair	filled with <u>despair</u>	
15. prairie	alone on the <u>prairie</u>	
16. chairperson	elected a <u>chairperson</u>	
17. ballet	danced in a <u>ballet</u>	
18. reign	to <u>reign</u> for eight years	
19. sleigh	a <u>sleigh</u> ride	
20. swaying	<u>swaying</u> in the wind	

Other Word Forms

> fail, failed
> frailness, frailty, frailer
> prevailed, prevailing
> avail, availed, availability
> praise
> awaited, awaiting
> regains
> contain
> entertain, entertainer
> acquainting, acquainted
> campaigning, campaigner
> affairs
> despaired
> prairies
> chairpersons
> ballets
> reigning
> sleighs
> sway, swayed

C. Challenge Words and Phrases

1. betrayed	<u>betrayed</u> by the spy
2. aquarium	freshwater <u>aquarium</u>
3. vibrations	<u>vibrations</u> of the strings
4. disobeyed	rarely <u>disobeyed</u>
5. pharaoh	laws of the <u>pharaoh</u>

D. Sort the _A_ Sounds All the words in the spelling list have a long _a_ or _ai_ with an _r_-controlled vowel sound. In alphabetical order, write the spelling words under the correct headings.

Long _a_ Sound Spelled _ai_

1. _____
2. _____
3. _____
4. _____
5. _____
6. _____
7. _____
8. _____
9. _____
10. _____
11. _____
12. _____

_ai_ with R-controlled Vowel Sound

13. _____
14. _____
15. _____
16. _____

Long _a_ Sound Spelled _ei_

17. _____
18. _____

Long _a_ Sound Spelled _ay_

19. _____

Long _a_ Sound Spelled _et_

20. _____

E. Break the Code Use the code to write the spelling words.

a	b	c	d	e	f	g	h	i	j	k	l	m	n	o	p	q	r	s	t	u	v	w	x	y	z
↓	↓	↓	↓	↓	↓	↓	↓	↓	↓	↓	↓	↓	↓	↓	↓	↓	↓	↓	↓	↓	↓	↓	↓	↓	↓
g	t	f	s	n	r	d	q	c	p	b	o	a	z	m	e	l	y	x	j	k	w	i	v	h	u

1. fpwae
2. jfmwdwea
3. cmwqzfp
4. mihzmweb
5. kmqqpb
6. mxmwqmkqp
7. iymwfjpfdle
8. dvmrwea
9. jfpxmwq
10. mccmwf
11. dqpway
12. imojmwae
13. ilebmwepf
14. mihzmwebmeip
15. cfmwq
16. mvmwb
17. fpamwe
18. pebpfbmweopeb
19. jfmwfwp
20. gpdjmwf

Spelling Words

failure frail prevail available praising await regain container entertainment acquaint acquaintance campaign affair despair prairie chairperson ballet reign sleigh swaying

F. Complete the Equations Write each of the spelling words to complete the equations. (The sign ≠ means "does not equal.") If you need help, use the **Spelling Dictionary**.

1. flimsy =
2. forest ≠
3. get back again =
4. on hand =
5. make familiar =
6. rule =
7. success ≠
8. swinging =
9. dance =
10. run for office =

11. committee leader =
12. hope ≠
13. holder =
14. succeed =
15. someone you have met =
16. criticizing ≠
17. amusement =
18. formal occasion =
19. sled =
20. expect =

G. Word Operations Add suffixes to the following base words to write spelling words or Other Word Forms (p. 4). For one word, you need to subtract a letter before adding the suffix.

	Base Words	Suffixes
1.	acquaint	ance
2.	fail	ure
3.	avail	able
4.	entertain	ment
5.	contain	er
6.	praise	ing
7.	sway	ing
8.	campaign	er
9.	await	ed
10.	regain	s
11.	reign	ing
12.	prevail	ed
13.	frail	er

H. Using Other Word Forms
Write the Other Word Form that completes each series.

1. prevail, _____ , prevailing
2. avail, _____ , availing
3. campaign, campaigned, _____
4. acquaint, acquainted, _____
5. despair, _____ , despairing

I. Challenge Words
Write the Challenge Word that completes each analogy.

betrayed	aquarium	vibrations	disobeyed	pharaoh

1. **Russian** is to **czar** as **Egyptian** is to _____
2. **patriot** is to **defended** as **traitor** is to _____
3. **earthquakes** is to **tremors** as **tuning forks** is to _____
4. **birds** is to **aviary** as **fish** is to _____
5. **complied** is to **conform** as **disregarded** is to _____

J. Spelling and Writing
Write each set of words in a sentence. You may use Other Word Forms. Proofread your work.

Example: sleigh – swaying – prairie — *The sleigh was swaying as we crossed the snowy prairie.*

1. despair – await – failure
2. ballet – acquaint – entertainment
3. chairperson – reign – affair
4. frail – prevail – regain
5. praising – acquaintance – campaign
6. sleigh – available – prairie
7. container – aquarium – failed
8. swaying – vibrations – awaited
9. betrayed – pharaoh – disobeyed

2

A. Pretest and Proofreading

B. Spelling Words and Phrases

1. easily — easily upset
2. grease — grease on the floor
3. displease — to displease a friend
4. meanness — selfishness and meanness
5. repeatedly — called repeatedly
6. weary — too weary to go
7. yearly — a yearly event
8. fearless — the fearless pilot
9. reality — fantasy or reality
10. seize — to seize the ball
11. ceiling — painted the ceiling
12. leisure — leisure time
13. receipt — signed the receipt
14. deceived — deceived by a trick
15. weird — a weird feeling
16. yield — to yield the way
17. grieve — will grieve the loss
18. relief — a sigh of relief
19. pierce — will pierce the balloon
20. fierce — fierce winds

Other Word Forms

ease, easy, easier
greasiest
please, displeasure
mean, meanest
repeat, repeating
wearied, wearily
year
fear, fearlessly
real, realities
seized
ceilings
leisurely
receive, receipts
deceive, deceit
weirdly, weirdness
yielded
grieving, grief
relieve, relieving
piercing
fiercely

C. Challenge Words and Phrases

1. reactions — tested the reactions
2. meandering — the meandering trail
3. perceived — perceived a flaw
4. southeastern — southeastern route
5. increasingly — increasingly difficult

D. Sort Your Vowels Write the twenty spelling words in alphabetical order. Put a wavy line under each *ea* word. Circle each *ie* word. Put an **X** before each *ei* word.

E. Sort Your *E* Sounds Use *ie* or *ei* to form spelling words. Write the words.

1. f __ __ rce

2. y __ __ ld

3. s __ __ ze

4. rec __ __ pt

5. c __ __ ling

6. p __ __ rce

7. rel __ __ f

8. w __ __ rd

9. l __ __ sure

10. dec __ __ ved

11. gr __ __ ve

F. Word Addition Complete each puzzle to find a word from the spelling list. Write the word.

1. y + not late = annually

2. abbreviation for *representative* + chew + edly = again

3. f + without hearing organs = brave

4. gr + comfort = oily substance

5. put on + y = tired

6. dis + make happy = disappoint

7. not fake + ity = fact

8. being cruel + ness = ill will

9. comfort − e + ily = effortlessly

Spelling Words

	easily grease displease meanness repeatedly weary yearly receipt fearless reality deceived seize weird ceiling leisure relief yield grieve pierce fierce

G. Words and Meanings Write a spelling word for each meaning. Then read down each column to find one spelling word and one Other Word Form (p. 8). Check your answers in the **Spelling Dictionary**.

1. mysterious   _ _ _ _☐_

2. with ease   ☐_ _ _ _ _ _

3. to annoy   _ _ _☐_ _ _

4. to make a hole in   _ _☐_ _ _

5. cruelty   _ _☐_ _ _ _

6. sales slip   _ _ _ _ _ _☐

7. oily substance   _ _☐_ _ _

8. fooled   _ _ _ _ _ _ _☐_

9. free time   ☐_ _ _ _ _ _

10. to give in   ☐_ _ _ _

11. an end to pain   _ _ _ _ _☐

12. to grab   _ _☐_ _

13. unafraid   _ _ _ _ _ _☐

14. to feel very sad   _☐_ _ _ _

15. a room's top part   ☐_ _ _ _ _ _

16. very tired   _☐_ _ _

17. actual fact   _ _ _☐_ _ _

18. annually   _ _ _ _ _ _☐

19. Write the spelling word and the Other Word Form made by the sets of boxes.

H. Using Other Word Forms
Add an ending to each adjective to make it an adverb. Then write this Other Word Form to complete each phrase.

Adjective   **Adverb**

1. leisure   stroll _____ down the path

2. weird   acted _____ in class

3. fierce   fought _____ in the ring

4. fearless   entered the old house _____

5. weary   finished the test _____

I. Challenge Words
Write the Challenge Word that completes each sentence.

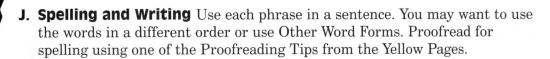

reactions	meandering	perceived	southeastern	increasingly

1. Sometimes we are _____ to be different than we really are.

2. The _____ river winds its way slowly toward the ocean.

3. The weather has become _____ colder.

4. The town is located in the _____ part of the state.

5. Their _____ to the news were unexpected.

J. Spelling and Writing
Use each phrase in a sentence. You may want to use the words in a different order or use Other Word Forms. Proofread for spelling using one of the Proofreading Tips from the Yellow Pages.

> Example: the <u>weary</u> traveler
> The <u>weary</u> traveler checked into the motel.

1. was <u>easily</u> mistaken

2. a <u>grease</u> spot

3. may <u>displease</u> the boss

4. the <u>meanness</u> of the dog

5. knocked <u>repeatedly</u>

6. the <u>weary</u> traveler

7. pays <u>yearly</u> dues

8. brave and <u>fearless</u>

9. must deal with <u>reality</u>

10. <u>seize</u> the land

11. a new <u>ceiling</u>

12. a man of <u>leisure</u>

13. signed the <u>receipt</u>

14. <u>deceived</u> the buyer

15. <u>weird</u> creatures

16. must <u>yield</u> the way

17. a place to <u>grieve</u>

18. <u>relief</u> from the <u>fierce</u> storm

3

A. Pretest and Proofreading

B. Spelling Words and Phrases

1. prime — of <u>prime</u> importance
2. likeliest — <u>likeliest</u> choice
3. guidance — will need <u>guidance</u>
4. tireless — <u>tireless</u> patience
5. aisle — darkened <u>aisle</u>
6. icicle — melting <u>icicle</u>
7. irony — cruel <u>irony</u>
8. giant — <u>giant</u> leap
9. fiber — a rug's <u>fiber</u>
10. fiery — over the <u>fiery</u> hurdle
11. library — worked at the <u>library</u>
12. license — driver's <u>license</u>
13. dinosaur — a <u>dinosaur</u> bone
14. violent — <u>violent</u> storm
15. briar — hid in the <u>briar</u> patch
16. climax — a book's <u>climax</u>
17. triumph — <u>triumph</u> or failure
18. science — <u>science</u> lab
19. scientist — a research <u>scientist</u>
20. hindsight — wiser with <u>hindsight</u>

Other Word Forms

primes, primed
like, likely
guide
tire, tirelessly
aisles
ice, icy, icicles
ironies, ironic
giants
fibers, fibrous
fire, fieriness
libraries
licensed, licensing
dinosaurs
violently, violence
briars
climaxes
triumphed, triumphant
sciences, scientific,
   scientists

C. Challenge Words and Phrases

1. prescribed — the <u>prescribed</u> amount
2. diagrams — sketches and <u>diagrams</u>
3. identification — lost her <u>identification</u>
4. librarian — asked the <u>librarian</u>
5. triangular — circular or <u>triangular</u>

D. Sort Your Words Write the twenty spelling words in alphabetical order. Put a check before the words with one syllable. Put an **X** before the words with two syllables. Circle the words with three syllables.

E. Context Clues Write a word from the spelling list to complete each sentence.

1. The thick _____ of the cloth makes it last.
2. The student needed _____ in choosing a topic.
3. I have to go to the _____ to return some books.
4. The play's surprising _____ was very dramatic.
5. The usher took us down the _____ to our seats.
6. Do you have a learner's permit or a _____ ?
7. The athlete was _____ after finishing the fifth lap.
8. That last win was a real _____ for our team.
9. I had to take a _____ step to cross over the wide stream.
10. My favorite subject is _____ .
11. The archeologist discovered some _____ fossils.
12. The _____ blaze from the volcano burned for several days.
13. The sun shone on the _____ , making it look like glass.
14. A hurricane is a sudden, sometimes _____ storm.
15. A twist of fate gave a sense of _____ to the story.
16. Taxation will be a _____ issue in the election.
17. The rabbit was once again found in the _____ patch.
18. The _____ wanted new laboratory equipment.
19. On a hot day, the _____ place to find me would be the beach.
20. In _____ we realized what had been our mistake.

Spelling Words

prime likeliest guidance tireless aisle icicle
irony giant fiber fiery library license
dinosaur violent briar climax triumph
science scientist hindsight

F. Crossword Puzzle Solve the puzzle by writing all the words from the spelling list. Check your answers in the **Spelling Dictionary**.

Across
1. most probable
4. a legal permit
8. an extinct reptile
9. advice
12. thread or material
14. huge
15. victory
17. a room or building for books
18. a pathway
19. knowledge based on observed facts

Down
2. unexpected outcome
3. a person trained in some science
5. the ability to see what should have been done, after something is over
6. a stick of ice
7. first in importance
10. a story's most exciting part
11. not tiring easily
12. hot
13. showing powerful force
16. a thorny bush

G. Using Other Word Forms Add an ending to each noun to make it an adjective. Then write this Other Word form to complete each phrase.

	Noun	Adjective
1.	irony	an _____ turn of events
2.	fiber	the _____ tissue of the cell
3.	triumph	a _____ march on the enemy
4.	science	the _____ method
5.	license	a _____ driver

H. Challenge Words Write the Challenge Word that completes each sentence.

prescribed	diagrams	identification	librarian	triangular

1. If the shape has three sides, it may be _____ .
2. If the patient needs medicine, it will be _____ by the doctor.
3. If he catalogs books, he may be a _____ .
4. If she is an illustrator, she may draw _____ .
5. If the customer is unknown, the clerk may ask for _____ .

I. Spelling and Writing Write *two* or more answers to each question. Use as many Spelling Words, Other Word Forms, and Challenge Words as you can. A few words are suggested. Proofread your work.

1. If you were an inventor of board games, what would your next game be like?
prime – likeliest – diagram – triangular – climax – triumph
Example: *The prime goal would be to complete three triangular paths.*

2. What would you do if you could travel millions of years back in time?
giant – dinosaur – science – identification – violent – scientist

3. What would you do if you had forgotten about a research report that is due tomorrow?
aisle – librarian – guidance – library – irony – tireless

4

A. Pretest and Proofreading

B. Spelling Words and Phrases

1. quote — a direct <u>quote</u>
2. dosage — increased the <u>dosage</u>
3. loneliness — never knew <u>loneliness</u>
4. dispose — to <u>dispose</u> of your trash
5. compose — a song to <u>compose</u>
6. oppose — to <u>oppose</u> war
7. suppose — <u>suppose</u> they won't
8. proposed — <u>proposed</u> a plan
9. exposure — <u>exposure</u> to heat
10. explode — will <u>explode</u> with anger
11. robot — a talking <u>robot</u>
12. gopher — <u>gopher</u> hole
13. social — a <u>social</u> occasion
14. locally — sold <u>locally</u>
15. notifies — <u>notifies</u> the police
16. proclaim — will <u>proclaim</u> a holiday
17. swollen — <u>swollen</u> glands
18. trophy — <u>trophy</u> on the shelf
19. molten — <u>molten</u> lava
20. revolt — staged a <u>revolt</u>

Other Word Forms

quoted, quotation
dose, dosages
lone, lonely
disposing, disposal
composing, composition
opposed, opposite, opposition
supposedly
propose, proposal
expose, exposing
explosion
robots
gophers
society, socially
local
notify
proclaiming
swell, swelled
trophies
melt
revolts, revolution

C. Challenge Words and Phrases

1. corrosion — weakened by <u>corrosion</u>
2. locomotive — old steam <u>locomotive</u>
3. quotient — calculate the <u>quotient</u>
4. radioactive — <u>radioactive</u> waste
5. microscopes — lenses of <u>microscopes</u>

D. Sort Your *O*'s Each of the words in the spelling list has a long *o* sound. In alphabetical order, write the spelling words to fit the correct headings.

Long *o* in the First or Only Syllable		Long *o* in the Second Syllable	
1. ____	7. ____	13. ____	17. ____
2. ____	8. ____	14. ____	18. ____
3. ____	9. ____	15. ____	19. ____
4. ____	10. ____	16. ____	20. ____
5. ____	11. ____		
6. ____	12. ____		

E. Generally Speaking Write the spelling word for the group it best fits.

1. award, prize, ____
2. nearby, not far, ____
3. tells, informs, ____
4. create, write, ____
5. burst, blow up, ____
6. hot, bubbly, ____
7. puffy, bruised, ____
8. squirrel, mole, ____
9. assume, expect, ____
10. sunburn, frostbite, ____

11. revolution, rebellion, ____
12. amount, prescription, ____
13. suggested, offered, ____
14. be against, dislike, ____
15. direct words, speech, ____
16. get rid of, throw out, ____
17. machine, computer, ____
18. sadness, isolation, ____
19. declare, announce, ____
20. friendly, talkative, ____

Spelling Words

quote	dosage	loneliness	dispose	compose	oppose
suppose	proposed	exposure	explode	robot	gopher
social	locally	notifies	proclaim	swollen	
trophy	molten	revolt			

F. Guide Words These word pairs are guide words that might appear in a dictionary. Write the words from the spelling list that would appear on the same page as each pair of guide words.

Example:

able – aisle

abstract

agency

compete – continue

1. _____

definition – disturbance

2. _____

domestic – equip

3. _____

equipment – extreme

4. _____   5. _____

generate – harried

6. _____

linger – memorable

7. _____   8. _____

memorial – neglect

9. _____

negligence – organize

10. _____   11. _____

process – qualify

12. _____   13. _____

quality – remember

14. _____

remembrance – scaling

15. _____   16. _____

slumber – summon

17. _____

suppose – uncommon

18. _____   20. _____

19. _____

G. Using Other Word Forms
Add an ending to each verb to make it a noun. Then write this Other Word Form to complete each phrase.

Verb	Noun
1. to quote	wrote a direct _____
2. to revolt	fought in the _____
3. to compose	wrote a long _____
4. to explode	heard the loud _____
5. to oppose	a member of the _____

H. Challenge Words
Write the Challenge Word that fits each group of words.

corrosion	locomotive	quotient	radioactive	microscopes

1. atoms, radium, nuclear, _____

2. metal, oxygen, rust, _____

3. magnify, instruments, biologist, _____

4. track, train, engineer, _____

5. division, dividend, answer, _____

I. Spelling and Writing
Write two or more questions about each statement. Use as many Spelling Words, Other Word Forms, and Challenge Words as you can. A few words are suggested. Proofread for spelling using one of the Proofreading Tips from the Yellow Pages.

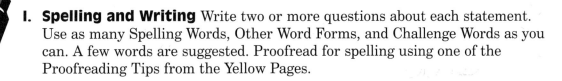

Example: The governor announced his engagement.
proposed   society   locally   suppose   notifies

Do you <u>suppose</u> he has to <u>notify</u> the <u>society</u> editor?
After his <u>proposal</u>, will they be married <u>locally</u>?

1. Automatic cameras are used to photograph volcanoes.
robot   molten   loneliness   exposure   explode   corrosion

2. A combination of treatments may be prescribed to fight cancer.
dosages   explosion   suppose   proposed   dispose   swollen
microscopes   radioactive

3. To get media attention, they planned a disturbance.
revolt   trophy   locally   social   notify   compose   oppose   proclaim

5

A. Pretest and Proofreading

B. Spelling Words and Phrases

1. accuse — might <u>accuse</u> me
2. misuse — won't <u>misuse</u> the tool
3. unite — will <u>unite</u> for freedom
4. unusual — an <u>unusual</u> laugh
5. museum — baseball <u>museum</u>
6. peculiar — <u>peculiar</u> behavior
7. commuter — <u>commuter</u> on the train
8. communities — urban <u>communities</u>
9. communication — <u>communication</u> center
10. juiciest — the <u>juiciest</u> orange
11. furious — calm or <u>furious</u>
12. assure — will <u>assure</u> success
13. feature — a strange <u>feature</u>
14. feeble — weak and <u>feeble</u>
15. sneeze — makes me <u>sneeze</u>
16. biweekly — <u>biweekly</u> newspaper
17. exceedingly — <u>exceedingly</u> slow
18. bacteria — disease-causing <u>bacteria</u>
19. career — <u>career</u> in computers
20. mosquitoes — buzzing <u>mosquitoes</u>

C. Challenge Words and Phrases

1. engineering — school of <u>engineering</u>
2. kangaroo — a leaping <u>kangaroo</u>
3. uranium — uses of <u>uranium</u>
4. altitude — the airplane's <u>altitude</u>
5. curiosity — <u>curiosity</u> of a child

Other Word Forms

accuses, accusing
use, misused
united, uniting, unify
usual, unusually
museums
peculiarly
commute, commuters
community
communicate
juice, juicy, juicier
fury, furiously
assuring, assuredly,
   assurance
features, featuring
feebly
sneezed, sneezing
week, weekly
exceed, exceeding
bacterium
careers
mosquito

D. Word Search The spelling words can be found in the word puzzle. The words appear across, down, and diagonally. Write the words.

Across

1.
2.
3.
4.
5.
6.
7.
8.

Down

9.
10.
11.
12.
13.
14.
15.

16.
17.
18.
19.

Diagonally

20.

```
e c o m m u n i t i e s u f
d o d u c s m e p d x e r u
m m o s q u i t a n c p i r
o m r e c h s c a r e e r i
s u r u l l u n l a e c u o
q n d m q u s w i c d u x u
u i e r s m e m e c i l u s
i c f e a t u r e u n i n a
t a u d z u p r n s g a u s
o t n f e e b l e e l r s s
e i i b i w e e k l y z u u
s o t c o m m u t e r y a r
x n e j u i c i e s t e l e
a c c u m e b a c t e r i a
```

E. What's the Suggestion? Write a word from the spelling list for each suggestion.

1. The word that suggests <u>neighborhoods</u>
2. The word that suggests <u>insects</u>
3. The word that suggests <u>rare</u>
4. The word that suggests <u>cough</u>
5. The word that suggests <u>promise</u>

Spelling Words

accuse   misuse   unite   unusual   museum
peculiar   commuter   communities   communication
juiciest   furious   assure   feature   feeble   sneeze
biweekly   exceedingly   bacteria   career   mosquitoes

F. What Am I? Write the spelling words to solve the puzzle. Read down the column to find Lindbergh's pride. All the words are in the spelling list. If you need help, use the **Spelling Dictionary**.

1. a place for exhibits _ _ ☐ _ _ _

2. odd or strange ☐ _ _ _ _ _ _ _

3. extremely _ _ _ _ _ _ ☐ _ _ _

4. life's work _ _ ☐ _ _ _

5. in a rage _ _ _ ☐ _ _ _

6. having the most liquid _ _ _ _ _ _ _ ☐

7. cities or towns _ ☐ _ _ _ _ _ _ _ _ _

8. an eye or a nose ☐ _ _ _ _ _ _

9. to blame _ _ _ _ ☐ _

10. to join together _ _ _ ☐ _

11. weak and fragile _ _ _ _ ☐ _

12. insects _ ☐ _ _ _ _ _ _ _

13. information sharing _ _ _ _ ☐ _ _ _ _ _ _ _

14. once every two weeks _ ☐ _ _ _ _ _

15. to handle incorrectly _ _ ☐ _ _ _

16. Write the name of Lindbergh's pride.

G. Using Other Word Forms Write the Other Word Form that completes each sentence.

1. The assignment was not completed in the regular way. It was finished most _____ (unusual).
2. He spoke very weakly. He used his voice _____ (feeble).
3. He said she was a liar. He is _____ (accuse) her of lying.
4. She spoke angrily. She answered _____ (furious).
5. She answered confidently. She responded _____ (assure).

H. Challenge Words Write the Challenge Word that completes each quotation.

engineering	kangaroo	uranium	altitude	curiosity

1. Teacher: "Encourage the natural _____ of every child."
2. Meteorologist: "The jet stream moves at a very high _____ ."
3. Scientist: "The radioactive element is called _____ ."
4. Zoo Keeper: "The pouch of a _____ is much like a pocket."
5. College Graduate: "I received my degree in _____ ."

I. Spelling and Writing Use each phrase in a sentence. You may want to use the words in a different order or use Other Word Forms. Proofread for spelling using one of the Proofreading Tips from the Yellow Pages.

1. may <u>accuse</u> them
2. did not <u>misuse</u> their power
3. <u>unite</u> the workers
4. <u>unusual</u> plants
5. the art <u>museum</u>
6. a <u>peculiar</u> idea
7. a daily <u>commuter</u>
8. live in <u>communities</u>
9. lines of <u>communication</u>
10. the <u>juiciest</u> fruit
11. the <u>furious</u> landlord
12. can <u>assure</u> you
13. <u>feature</u> the actor
14. a <u>feeble</u> excuse
15. caused me to <u>sneeze</u>
16. a <u>biweekly</u> magazine
17. <u>exceedingly</u> fast
18. microscopic <u>bacteria</u>
19. a <u>career</u> move
20. bitten by <u>mosquitoes</u>

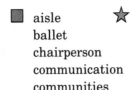

REVIEWING LESSONS 1-5

■ aisle	★ deceived	▲ irony	◆ praising	○ swaying
ballet	dosage	likeliest	prime	swollen
chairperson	exceedingly	locally	proposed	triumph
communication	exposure	loneliness	reality	weird
communities	fiery	prairie	suppose	yield

A. Slash Away Remove one letter from each word. Join the remaining letters to write an Other Word Form for each spelling word. If you need help, use the **Spelling Dictionary**.

Example: saw bells = ○ ___*swells*___

1. bald let ring an = ■ _____

2. awe bird on mess = ○ _____

3. red ail = ◆ _____

4. pray his wed = ◆ _____

5. props of sings = ◆ _____

6. lot calf city = ▲ _____

7. up trim her = ◆ _____

8. chairs perk is ones = ■ _____

9. yip weld fed = ○ _____

10. deck me living = ★ _____

11. aim as lets = ■ _____

12. come me run city = ■ _____

13. saw day bed = ○ _____

14. alone sob met = ▲ _____

15. pray it or ties = ▲ _____

16. sir ton tic = ▲ _____

17. does aged as = ★ _____

18. try is bump hand it = ○ _____

19. we ax ace beds = ★ _____

20. lick rely = ▲ _____

21. sum opposed lay = ◆ _____

22. come me pun tic rate = ■ _____

23. fin are = ★ _____

24. me ax prose = ★ _____

failure	displease	yearly	trophy	hindsight
available	meanness	guidance	biweekly	container
acquaintance	repeatedly	scientist	career	entertainment
easily	library	quote	mosquitoes	molten
relief	notifies	commuter	explode	juiciest

B. Word Clues Write the spelling word that goes with each clue. Then write an Other Word Form for all but one spelling word. If you need help, use the **Spelling Dictionary**.

1. in every year

2. having the most liquid

3. insects that bite humans

4. again and again

5. someone's exact words

6. able to be obtained

7. a jar to hold something

8. a place to house books

9. happening every two weeks

10. opposite of foresight

11. with little effort

12. one who travels daily

13. amusement

14. to offend

15. a lack of success

16. direction

17. known only slightly

18. made a liquid by heating

19. a profession

20. informs

21. the removal of anxiety

22. a prize

23. unkindness

24. to burst forth suddenly

25. one learned in science

■ sleigh	★ fearless	▲ compose	◆ briar	● museum
misuse	seize	gopher	feeble	affair
grease	fierce	dispose	bacteria	pierce
weary	dinosaur	license	unite	revolt
grieve	science	icicle	ceiling	giant

C. **Newspaper Headlines** Write Other Word Forms or the spelling words to complete the newspaper headlines. Write each word or its Other Word Form only once. Capitalize each word. If you need help, use the **Spelling Dictionary**.

1. Lions Surprised When Tamer Roars ★ _____
2. Banana Import Company ★ _____ by Chimpanzees
3. Ear ● _____ Leaves Holes in Head
4. Pets Find Owners ● _____
5. Field Mice and ▲ _____ Meet Over Territorial Dispute
6. Worker Bees ◆ _____ to Defeat Drones
7. Cinderella Arrives in Pumpkin for a Formal ● _____
8. Flighty Fowl Flees ★ _____ From Foe
9. ▲ _____ Clothing Becomes Newest Fad
10. Fish Found ◆ _____ Floundering for Food
11. Poorly Wired Lamps on ◆ _____ Cause Shocking Effect
12. Mad ★ _____ Guilty of Guinea Pigs' Escape
13. Little ▲ _____ Required for Driving Miniature Cars
14. Wax ● _____ Close Due to Candle Shortage
15. Hare-raising Adventure Occurs in ◆ _____ Patch
16. Jack Meets Two ● _____ at End of Beanstalk
17. ■ _____ Exits Become Entrances
18. Charlie Brown Is ■ _____ -stricken Over Team's Poor Record
19. Dozens of ★ _____ Dine in Den
20. Under the In-FLU-ence of a ◆ _____ Virus
21. Jack and Jill Show No Signs of ■ _____ After Climb
22. Staff ▲ _____ New Songs
23. Reindeer Without Goggles Causes ■ _____ Mishap
24. Nature's ▲ _____ Are Arctic Poles
25. Turtle ■ _____ Roadway to Increase Speed

R E V I E W

accuse	climax	furious	proclaim	sneeze
acquaint	despair	leisure	receipt	social
assure	feature	oppose	regain	tireless
await	fiber	peculiar	reign	unusual
campaign	frail	prevail	robot	violent

D. Suffix Countdown Add suffixes to the spelling words as indicated below. Once a word is used it cannot be used again. Check your answers in the **Spelling Dictionary**.

1. The Suffix *ous*
   Add the suffix *ous* to the word *fiber* and write the word. Note the spelling change.

2. The Suffix *ly*
   Add the suffix *ly* to eight words on the list that do not undergo a spelling change when *ly* is added. Write the words.

3. The Suffix *ing*
   Add the suffix *ing* to five other words on the list that drop the final *e* before adding *ing*. Write the words.

4. The Suffix *ed*
   Add the suffix *ed* to nine other words that do not undergo a spelling change when *ed* is added. Write the words.

5. The Suffix *s*
   Add the suffix *s* to the two remaining words. Write the words.

7

A. Pretest and Proofreading

B. Spelling Words and Phrases

1. **phrase** — phrase or sentence
2. **scaling** — scaling the mountain
3. **engage** — to engage in conversation
4. **disgrace** — left in disgrace
5. **create** — to create a design
6. **refrigerator** — message on the refrigerator
7. **persuade** — ability to persuade
8. **persuasive** — persuasive argument
9. **agency** — ad agency
10. **ablest** — ablest person
11. **ancient** — ancient ruins
12. **patient** — to assist the patient
13. **patience** — lost my patience
14. **fatal** — fatal accident
15. **gracious** — gracious behavior
16. **stationery** — printed stationery
17. **occasion** — an occasion to remember
18. **combination** — a combination of colors
19. **publication** — a recent publication
20. **contrary** — contrary to fact

Other Word Forms

phrasing
scale
engaged, engaging
disgraced, disgraceful
created
refrigerate, refrigeration
persuaded, persuading, persuasively
agent, agencies
able
ancients, ancientness
patients, patiently
fate, fatally
grace, graceful
occasional
combine, combined
public, publicity, publish
contrarily, contrariness

C. Challenge Words and Phrases

1. **imitation** — an excellent imitation
2. **immigration** — immigration into a country
3. **recreation** — rest and recreation
4. **patriotic** — a patriotic speech
5. **stockade** — protected by a stockade

D. Word Search The spelling words can be found in the word puzzle. The words appear across, down, and diagonally. Write the words.

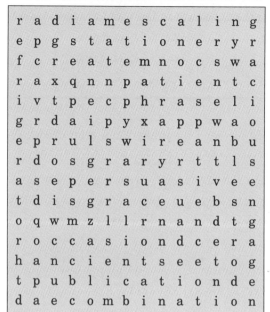

```
r a d i a m e s c a l i n g
e p g s t a t i o n e r y r
f c r e a t e m n o c s w a
r a x q n n p a t i e n t c
i v t p e c p h r a s e l i
g r d a i p y x a p p w a o
e p r u l s w i r e a n b u
r d o s g r a r y r t t l s
a s e p e r s u a s i v e e
t d i s g r a c e u e b s n
o q w m z l l r n a n d t g
r o c c a s i o n d c e r a
h a n c i e n t s e e t o g
t p u b l i c a t i o n d e
d a e c o m b i n a t i o n
```

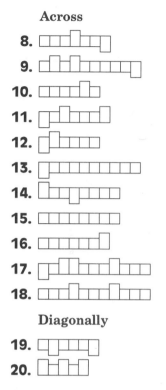

Across

8.
9.
10.
11.
12.
13.
14.
15.
16.
17.
18.

Diagonally

19.
20.

Down

1.
2.
3.
4.

5.
6.
7.

E. Guide Words These word pairs are guide words that might appear in a dictionary. Write the words from the spelling list that would appear on the same page as each pair of guide words.

able–define		domestic–harried		personal–qualify	
1. _____	4. _____	8. _____	10. _____	14. _____	16. _____
2. _____	5. _____	9. _____		15. _____	17. _____
3. _____	6. _____				

definition–disturbance	negligence–patient		quality–summon	
7. _____	11. _____	13. _____	18. _____	20. _____
	12. _____		19. _____	

Spelling Words

phrase	scaling	engage	disgrace	create	refrigerator
persuade	persuasive	agency	ablest	ancient	
patient	patience	fatal	gracious	stationery	
occasion	combination	publication	contrary		

F. Words and Meanings Write a spelling word for each meaning. Then read down each column to find three more spelling words.

1. most capable   _ _ _ ☐ _ _

2. very old   _ ☐ _ _ _ _ _

3. charming   ☐ _ _ _ _ _ _ _

4. convince   _ _ _ _ _ ☐ _ _

5. a service organization   _ ☐ _ _ _ _

6. writing paper   _ _ _ _ _ _ ☐ _ _

7. shame   _ _ _ _ _ _ ☐ _

8. part of a sentence   _ _ ☐ _ _ _

9. an ill person   _ _ _ _ ☐ _ _

10. a mixture   _ _ _ _ _ _ ☐ _ _ _

11. published material   _ _ _ _ _ _ _ ☐ _ _ _

12. convincing   _ _ _ _ _ _ _ _ ☐ _

13. a machine that keeps food cold   _ _ ☐ _ _ _ _ _ _ _ _ _

14. willingness to wait   _ ☐ _ _ _ _ _ _

15. opposite   _ _ _ ☐ _ _ _ _

16. a special event   _ _ _ ☐ _ _ _ _

17. climbing a steep hill   _ _ _ ☐ _ _ _

18. Write the three spelling words made by the sets of boxes.

G. Using Other Word Forms Write the Other Word Form that completes each sentence.

1. The word _____ (refrigerator) means keeping things cold.
2. The word _____ (patient) means in a calm manner.
3. The word _____ (disgrace) means shameful.
4. The word _____ (occasion) means random or infrequent.
5. The word _____ (persuasive) means in a convincing manner.

H. Challenge Words Write the Challenge Word that replaces each underlined word or phrase.

imitation	immigration	recreation	patriotic	stockade

1. Bicycle riding is my favorite <u>fun activity</u>.
2. The soldiers stormed the walls of the <u>fort</u>.
3. She is <u>loyal to her country</u>.
4. Their <u>coming</u> to America was historically important.
5. A rhinestone is an <u>artificial</u> gem.

I. Spelling and Writing Write each set of words in a sentence. You may use Other Word Forms. Proofread your work.

1. combination – refrigerator – persuade
2. phrase – publication – agency
3. scaling – ancient – patience
4. occasion – disgrace – fatal
5. persuasive – patient – engage
6. gracious – stationery – contrary
7. ablest – create – imitation
8. stockade – patriotic – engaged
9. immigration – agencies – recreation

8

A. Pretest and Proofreading

B. Spelling Words and Phrases

1. scheme	shrewd <u>scheme</u>	
2. extreme	in <u>extreme</u> pain	
3. compete	eager to <u>compete</u>	
4. concrete	poured the <u>concrete</u>	
5. convene	must <u>convene</u> the meeting	
6. convenience	for your <u>convenience</u>	
7. legal	a <u>legal</u> contract	
8. theory	a mathematical <u>theory</u>	
9. previous	<u>previous</u> month	
10. appreciate	to <u>appreciate</u> your help	
11. procedure	step-by-step <u>procedure</u>	
12. mere	a <u>mere</u> problem	
13. cereal	hot <u>cereal</u>	
14. experience	<u>experience</u> and training	
15. mysterious	<u>mysterious</u> sounds	
16. interior	<u>interior</u> design	
17. interfere	won't <u>interfere</u>	
18. skiing	skating or <u>skiing</u>	
19. policy	insurance <u>policy</u>	
20. England	flew to <u>England</u>	

Other Word Forms

schemed, scheming
extremely
competing, competition
concreteness
convened, convention
convenient
legally, legalize
theories
previously
appreciated, appreciation
proceed, procedures
merely
cereals
experiencing
mystery, mysteries
interiors
interference, interferes, interfering
ski, skied
policies
English

C. Challenge Words and Phrases

1. pyramids	photographed the <u>pyramids</u>
2. prefixes	a list of <u>prefixes</u>
3. hemisphere	one <u>hemisphere</u>
4. frequency	<u>frequency</u> of errors
5. tedious	a <u>tedious</u> task

D. Break the Code Use the code to write the spelling words.

a	b	c	d	e	f	g	h	i	j	k	l	m	n	o	p	q	r	s	t	u	v	w	x	y	z
↓	↓	↓	↓	↓	↓	↓	↓	↓	↓	↓	↓	↓	↓	↓	↓	↓	↓	↓	↓	↓	↓	↓	↓	↓	↓
g	z	q	w	s	v	e	a	n	x	y	i	f	j	p	u	l	b	k	c	d	r	t	h	m	o

1. liwgvmgvg
2. ykewgvlzpe
3. esllia
4. ygvg
5. gjwvgyg
6. hoovgtlhwg
7. qgahq
8. ovgflzpe
9. tzitvgwg
10. wxgzvk
11. giaqhiu
12. gjogvlgitg
13. etxgyg
14. tzyogwg
15. tgvghq
16. tzifgilgitg
17. ozqltk
18. liwgvlzv
19. ovztgupvg
20. tzifgig

E. Base Words The spelling list contains seventeen base words and three words that are not base words. Write each spelling word.

Words That Are Not Base Words	Base Words	Words That Are Not Base Words	Base Words
1. merely	_____	11. theories	_____
2. schemed	_____	12. policies	_____
3. extremely	_____	13. interiors	_____
4. convened	_____	14. appreciated	_____
5. competing	_____	15. experiencing	_____
6. interferes	_____	16. concreteness	_____
7. English	_____	17. _____	convenient
8. previously	_____	18. _____	mystery
9. cereals	_____	19. _____	proceed
10. legally	_____	20. _____	ski

Spelling Words

scheme extreme compete concrete convene
convenience legal theory previous appreciate
procedure mere cereal experience mysterious
interior interfere skiing policy England

F. Cause and Effect Write a word from the spelling list to complete each sentence.

1. If you painted the inside of the house, you redecorated the _____ .
2. If you traveled through Great Britain, you visited _____ .
3. If you refuse to be involved, you will not _____ .
4. If the judge is ready, the clerk will _____ the court.
5. If it's a cement material for construction, it must be _____ .
6. If the decision is lawful, it must be _____ .
7. If it's not a fact, it could be just a guess, or _____ .
8. If you like oatmeal and bran flakes, you probably enjoy _____ .
9. If you follow the directions strictly, you follow a step-by-step _____ .
10. If you enter the race, you will _____ .
11. If you thanked me for my help, you must _____ my efforts.
12. If you are a downhill racer, you enjoy _____ .
13. If you purchased an insurance plan, you will receive a _____ .
14. If you require a precise plan of action, you need a foolproof _____ .
15. If you work at many jobs, you will gain much _____ .
16. If Ulysses was not a god, he must have been a _____ mortal.
17. If the pressure is very intense, it must be _____ .
18. If an appliance gives you more free time, it is a great _____ .
19. If you waited on tables before, you have had _____ restaurant experience.
20. If you see strange lights in the sky, you may be viewing a _____ event.

G. Using Other Word Forms Write the Other Word Form that completes each sentence.

1. The _____ (compete) between the teams was fierce.
2. The political _____ (convene) was held in Atlantic City, NJ.
3. The referee called a penalty for _____ (interfere).
4. The school's _____ (policy) were best for the students.
5. She showed her _____ (appreciate) by applauding.

H. Challenge Words Write the Challenge Word that completes each sentence.

pyramids	prefixes	hemisphere	frequency	tedious

1. If the land is above the equator, it is in the northern _____ .
2. If they're Egyptian tombs, they may be _____ .
3. If the job is tiring and boring, it is probably _____ .
4. If an event happens often, it occurs with _____ .
5. If the word parts appear at the beginning, they may be _____ .

I. Spelling and Writing Write two or more questions about each statement. Use as many Spelling Words, Other Word Forms, and Challenge Words as you can. A few words are suggested. Proofread for spelling using one of the Proofreading Tips from the Yellow Pages.

1. A trip to Vermont in winter needs careful planning.
   extreme   skiing   England   cereal   interfere   compete

   Example: Is it always <u>extremely</u> cold in New <u>England</u>?

2. Amazing artifacts have been found in Egypt.
   pyramids   mysterious   interior   previous   concrete
      convenience   tedious

3. The town has made rules for in line skating and skateboarding.
   convene   legal   theory   appreciated   procedure   mere   policy

9

A. Pretest and Proofreading

B. Spelling Words and Phrases

1. **sigh** — a weary sigh
2. **knight** — a knight in armor
3. **mightiest** — mightiest or weakest
4. **aside** — would set aside
5. **resides** — resides in the city
6. **preside** — will preside at the meeting
7. **describe** — to describe the scene
8. **subscribe** — will subscribe to the paper
9. **confined** — confined by illness
10. **require** — will require proof
11. **acquired** — acquired great wealth
12. **trifle** — a trifle upset
13. **quietest** — quietest time of day
14. **society** — rules of society
15. **variety** — variety of colors
16. **deny** — will deny entrance
17. **apply** — to apply for the job
18. **hygiene** — personal hygiene
19. **linger** — to linger outside the door
20. **bestow** — will bestow the gifts

Other Word Forms

sighing
knights, knighted
might, mightier
asides
reside, resided
presiding
describing, description
subscribed, subscription
confine, confining
required, requirement
acquire, acquiring
trifles
quiet, quieter
social, societies
vary, varieties
denies, denying
applies
hygienic
lingering
bestowed

C. Challenge Words and Phrases

1. **hydrogen** — a hydrogen balloon
2. **entitled** — entitled to a share
3. **lightweight** — a lightweight tent
4. **perspires** — perspires when hot
5. **hibernate** — animals that hibernate

D. Sort Your Long *i*'s In alphabetical order, write the spelling words under the correct headings.

Long *i* Followed by a Consonant and Silent *e*		Long *i* Followed by a *gh* Combination		Long *i* Followed by Two Consonants and *e*
1. ____	5. ____	12. ____	14. ____	18. ____
2. ____	6. ____	13. ____		
3. ____	7. ____			
4. ____	8. ____	**The Letter *y* with the Sound of Long *i***		
Long *i* Followed by *e*		15. ____	17. ____	
9. ____	11. ____	16. ____		
10. ____				

19. Write the two words that did not fit under any heading.

E. Generally Speaking Write each spelling word for the group it best fits.

1. calmest, most silent, ____

2. smooth on, spread, ____

3. stay, leave slowly, ____

4. soldier, crusader, ____

5. obtained, gathered, ____

6. small amount, a bit, ____

7. apart, away from, ____

8. order, sign up for, ____

9. imprisoned, restricted, ____

10. refuse, not allow, ____

11. health, cleanliness, ____

12. strongest, bravest, ____

13. community, group, ____

14. assortment, different kinds, ____

15. lives, makes one's home, ____

16. tell, explain, ____

17. yawn, moan, ____

18. direct, lead, ____

19. give, present, ____

20. need, want, ____

Spelling Words

sigh knight mightiest aside resides preside
describe subscribe confined require acquired
trifle quietest society variety deny apply
hygiene linger bestow

F. Crossword Puzzle Solve the puzzle by writing all the words from the spelling list. Check your answers in the **Spelling Dictionary**.

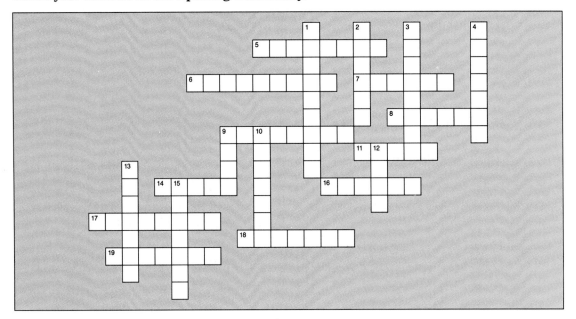

Across

5. obtained
6. strongest
7. a little bit
8. a soldier of the Middle Ages
9. to tell about something
11. to one side
14. to put on or spread on
16. to stay for a while
17. most silent
18. cleanliness
19. to need or want

Down

1. to order a magazine
2. to give as a gift
3. limited in movement
4. a number of different types
9. to state as untrue
10. a community
12. a sorrowful sound
13. makes one's home
15. to direct a meeting

G. Using Other Word Forms Write the Other Word Form that completes each sentence.

1. He gave a good explanation of its looks. He gave a _____ (describe) of it.
2. She was obtaining many pieces of real estate. She was _____ (acquired) property.
3. The garden had all kinds of plants. It was filled with many _____ (variety) of vegetables.
4. She reordered the magazine for another year. She renewed her _____ (subscribe).
5. The essay was necessary to enter the contest. It was a _____ (require).

H. Challenge Words Write the Challenge Word that completes each phrase.

hydrogen	entitled	lightweight	perspires	hibernate

1. either named or _____
2. either sleep or _____
3. either sweats or _____
4. either a featherweight or a _____
5. either a gas or _____

I. Spelling and Writing Write *two* or more answers to each question. Use as many Spelling Words, Other Word Forms, and Challenge Words as you can. A few words are suggested. Proofread your work.

1. What would you write about next if you were an author of a series of stories set in the Middle Ages?

   society – knight – preside – deny – trifle – bestow

2. What would you do if a friendly bear was wandering around your city or town just before winter set in?

   lightweight – hibernate – mightiest – describe – linger – sigh

3. How would you describe your neighborhood to a visitor from another planet?

   entitled – resides – aside – confined – quietest – variety

10

A. Pretest and Proofreading

B. Spelling Words and Phrases

1. **humane** — humane treatment
2. **sensation** — icy sensation
3. **notation** — wrote in notation form
4. **quotation** — quotation marks
5. **vocation** — to choose a vocation
6. **education** — further education
7. **aviation** — aviation school
8. **automation** — automation in the factory
9. **circulation** — circulation of air
10. **generation** — third generation
11. **limitation** — time limitation
12. **occupation** — my aunt's occupation
13. **civilization** — destroyed civilization
14. **conversation** — lively conversation
15. **consideration** — small consideration
16. **association** — joined the association
17. **administration** — administration offices
18. **imagination** — vivid imagination
19. **examination** — examination room
20. **destination** — had no destination

C. Challenge Words and Phrases

1. **agitation** — cause for agitation
2. **frustration** — showed frustration
3. **pronunciation** — the pronunciation key
4. **interpretation** — a different interpretation
5. **vaccination** — the vaccination records

Other Word Forms

human, humanely, humanity
sense, sensations
note, notated
quote
vocational
educate, educational
aviate
automate, automatic
circulate, circulating
generate, generated
limit
occupy, occupies
civil, civilized
converse
consider
associate
administer
image, imagine
examine
destine, destiny

D. Inform-ATION Answer these questions by writing an *ation* word from the spelling list. Use each word once.

What ATION . . .

1. is the study of flying?

2. is round and round?

3. is a job?

4. is thoughtfulness?

5. is received in school?

6. is someone else's words?

7. is a dialogue?

8. is a test?

9. is a feeling?

10. is the school principal?

11. is written in symbols?

12. restricts someone?

13. is the end?

14. is people of the same age?

15. is an organization?

16. is used in pretending?

17. is done by machines?

18. is a people with a developed culture?

19. What is the only word on the list that is not an *ation* word?

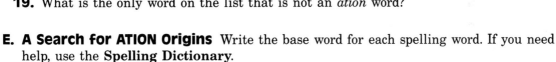

E. A Search for ATION Origins Write the base word for each spelling word. If you need help, use the **Spelling Dictionary**.

1. administration

2. association

3. automation

4. aviation

5. circulation

6. civilization

7. consideration

8. conversation

9. destination

10. education

11. examination

12. generation

13. imagination

14. limitation

15. notation

16. occupation

17. quotation

18. sensation

19. Write the two words not used.

Spelling Words

humane   sensation   notation   quotation   vocation
education   aviation   automation   circulation   generation
limitation   occupation   civilization   conversation
consideration   association   administration   imagination
examination   destination

F. Scrambled Words Unscramble the scrambled word to find the spelling word that completes the sentence. Write the word.

1. I'm saving for my college _____ (cudeatoin).

2. Use your _____ (amigianinot) to improve your composition.

3. The _____ (motininistrada) of the president lasted eight years.

4. Due to _____ (atouamoitn), our work is now done more quickly.

5. The newspaper has increased its _____ (tancoriclui) since last year.

6. The ancient Greek _____ (toniiiivlcaz) influenced architecture.

7. I am training for a _____ (anvocoit) in electronics.

8. The pilots started studying _____ (nataivoi) when they were sixteen.

9. My oldest cousin is of a different _____ (einregaont) than I.

10. Can you read this musical _____ (tantonoi)?

11. The final _____ (mixiaetonan) was easy because they studied.

12. What _____ (canuociopt) interests you for a career?

13. Your generosity shows you are very _____ (menhua).

14. The _____ (tootanqui) from the speech is on the last page.

15. The teachers' _____ (icinostasoa) will meet on Friday.

16. The carnival ride gave us a _____ (inesstoan) of dizziness.

17. After careful _____ (tiserdanoocni), we decided to buy a new car.

18. They had a brief phone _____ (vascoenrotin).

19. The parking meter has an hour's time _____ (nimitilato).

20. Our trip's final _____ (ioinsteadtn) is a secret.

G. Using Other Word Forms Write the Other Word Form that completes each sentence.

1. Medical research benefits all of _____ (humane).
2. Students learn different trades at _____ (vocation) schools.
3. She felt it was her _____ (destination) to become a doctor.
4. Our teacher encourages us to watch _____ (education) television programs.
5. The school song _____ (generation) a lot of school spirit.

H. Challenge Words Write the Challenge Word that completes each sentence.

agitation	frustration	pronunciation	interpretation	vaccination

1. Smallpox can be prevented through _____ .
2. Each word has its own special _____ .
3. I tried hard but finally stopped because of my _____ .
4. The coded message needs careful _____ .
5. Angry club members caused much _____ during the meeting.

I. Spelling and Writing Write *two* or more answers to each question. Use as many Spelling Words, Other Word Forms, and Challenge Words as you can. A few words are suggested. Proofread your work.

1. What would you do if you became lost on a trip through a foreign country?

   interpretation – pronunciation – destination – conversation – agitation – examination

2. If you were a historian living in the twenty-fifth century, how would you describe life back in the year A.D. 2000?

   civilization – automation – humane – education – vocation – imagination

3. How would you help a friend explain a mistake to his or her parents?

   generation – quotation – frustration – consideration – limitation – notation

11

A. Pretest and Proofreading

B. Spelling Words and Phrases

1. snoop — to <u>snoop</u> for a clue
2. groove — <u>groove</u> of the record
3. noodle — <u>noodle</u> soup
4. prune — to <u>prune</u> the trees
5. numeral — missing <u>numeral</u>
6. numerous — <u>numerous</u> choices
7. pursue — will <u>pursue</u> tirelessly
8. conclude — must <u>conclude</u> soon
9. conclusion — <u>conclusion</u> of the story
10. solution — found a <u>solution</u>
11. pollution — water <u>pollution</u>
12. constitution — signed the <u>constitution</u>
13. youth — <u>youth</u> center
14. nuisance — public <u>nuisance</u>
15. lieutenant — <u>lieutenant</u> or major
16. canoe — <u>canoe</u> paddle
17. endurance — <u>endurance</u> test
18. oyster — an <u>oyster</u> shell
19. joyous — a <u>joyous</u> occasion
20. moisture — covered with <u>moisture</u>

Other Word Forms

snooped, snooping
grooved
noodles
pruned, pruning
number, numerals,
    numerical
pursued, pursuing, pursuit
concluded, concluding,
    conclusions
solve, solutions
pollutant, pollute, polluted
constitute, constitutional
youthful
nuisances
lieutenants
canoed, canoeing
endure, endured, enduring
oysters
joy, joyful, joyously
moist, moisten

C. Challenge Words and Phrases

1. excluded — felt <u>excluded</u>
2. neutral — remained <u>neutral</u>
3. duplicated — cannot be <u>duplicated</u>
4. rendezvous — <u>rendezvous</u> in the park
5. nuclear — <u>nuclear</u> energy

D. Generally Speaking Write each spelling word for the group it best fits. You may wish to check the meanings of *conclude, conclusion,* and *solution* in the **Spelling Dictionary**.

1. spy, prowl, _____
2. strength, toughness, _____
3. laws, document, _____
4. decide, finish, _____
5. end, decision, _____
6. answer, explanation, _____
7. track, path, _____
8. clam, shellfish, _____
9. chase, follow, _____
10. rain, dew, _____
11. impurity, filth, _____
12. digit, integer, _____
13. trim, cut, _____
14. annoyance, bother, _____
15. many, considerable, _____
16. festive, merry, _____
17. child, youngster, _____
18. major, sergeant, _____
19. spaghetti, macaroni, _____
20. boat, raft, _____

Spelling Words

snoop groove noodle prune numeral numerous
pursue conclude conclusion solution pollution
constitution youth nuisance lieutenant canoe
endurance oyster joyous moisture

E. Crossword Puzzle Solve the puzzle by writing all the words from the spelling list. Check your answers in the **Spelling Dictionary**.

Across

2. to decide
3. a legal document
5. a shellfish
6. to spy
10. annoyance
12. the answer to a problem
14. feeling happy
15. a digit
16. a child
17. dew
18. a dried plum
19. a track

Down

1. many
3. a decision
4. macaroni
7. an officer
8. a type of rowboat
9. to chase
11. impurity or filth
13. lasting strength

F. Using Other Word Forms Write the Other Word Form that completes each series.

1. concludes, concluded, _____
2. prunes, _____, pruning
3. pursues, pursued, _____
4. endures, _____, enduring
5. canoes, canoed, _____

G. Challenge Words Write the Challenge Word that completes each analogy.

excluded	neutral	duplicated	rendezvous	nuclear

1. **sun** is to **solar** as **atom** is to _____
2. **accept** is to **reject** as **included** is to _____
3. **beach** is to **seashore** as **meeting** is to _____
4. **biased** is to **unbiased** as **taking sides** is to _____
5. **repeated** is to **reproduced** as **copied** is to _____

H. Spelling and Writing Write each set of words in a sentence. You may use Other Word Forms. Proofread for spelling using one of the Proofreading Tips from the Yellow Pages.

1. prune, noodle, oysters
2. solution, pollution, conclusion
3. nuisance, youth, snoop
4. lieutenant, groove, canoe
5. endurance, numerous, pursued
6. moisture, constitution, solution
7. numeral, solution, conclude
8. joyous, youth, noodle
9. concluding, endurance, moisture

12

■ patience	★ skiing	▲ experience	◆ moisture	○ mysterious
scaling	engage	aviation	compete	nuisance
convenience	prune	noodle	snoop	variety
refrigerator	destination	numeral	numerous	association
endurance	mightiest	quietest	England	persuasive

A. A Day in the Park Write Other Word Forms or the spelling words to complete these happenings that you may or may not see in a park. Write each Other Word Form only once. If you need help, use the **Spelling Dictionary**.

1. cats ■ _____ watching the birds

2. young ▲ _____ flying model airplanes

3. people ★ _____ in conversation

4. children ○ _____ their parents to let them swim

5. ankles tied together for ◆ _____ in a three-legged race

6. a family looking for a ■ _____ picnic spot

7. people ▲ _____ difficulty in finding a good picnic spot

8. food ○ _____ disappearing before it's been eaten

9. a motorboat pulling a ★ _____ on the lake

10. students doing their ◆ _____ lessons under a tree

11. fishermen weighing their catch on a ■ _____

12. sunbathers ■ _____ the hot rays

13. children watching ◆ _____ kites get caught in trees

14. a baby taking a nap ▲ _____ in the shade

15. an ant using all of its ★ _____ to carry a crumb

16. a picnic basket containing many ○ _____ of sandwiches

17. small coolers ■ _____ drinks and food

18. dance ○ _____ performing for free

19. squirrels ◆ _____ around for scraps of food

20. gardeners ★ _____ the bushes

21. children stringing hard ▲ _____ to make necklaces

22. runners wiping the ◆ _____ from their sneakers

23. a caller shouting out ▲ _____ for a bingo game

24. a busload of picnickers finally reaching its ★ _____

25. ants being ○ _____ on a picnic table

■ conclude	★ scheme	▲ linger	◆ legal	● deny
knight	policy	conversation	solution	education
persuade	patient	apply	phrase	stationery
disgrace	appreciate	constitution	oyster	subscribe
ablest	extreme	circulation	imagination	procedure

B. Puzzling Proverb

For each clue, write Other Word Forms for all but one spelling word.* Then use the boxed letters to complete the proverb. If you need help, use the **Spelling Dictionary**.

1. sea animals ◆ _ _ _ _□_ _ _
2. verses ◆ _□_ _ _ _ _
3. puts on ▲ _ _ _ _ _ _ _□
4. rules ★ _□_ _ _ _ _ _
5. refuses ● _ _ _□_ _ _
6. taught ●□_ _ _ _ _ _ _
*7. paper ● _ _ _ _ _□_ _ _
8. lawfully ◆ _ _□_ _ _
9. calmly ★ _□_ _ _ _ _ _
10. talking ▲ _ _ _ _ _□_ _ _
11. methods ● _ _□_ _ _ _ _
12. laws ▲ _ _ _ _ _ _ _□_ _
13. shameful ■ _ _ _ _ _ _ _□_ _
14. rotates ▲ _ _ _ _ _ _ _ _□_
15. valued ★ _ _ _ _ _ _ _ _□
16. dreaming ◆ _ _ _ _ _ _□_ _
17. exceptionally ★ _ _□_ _ _ _ _ _
18. answers ◆ _ _ _ _ _ _ _□_ _
19. capable ■ _ _ _ _□
20. bought ● _ _ _ _ _ _ _ _ _□
21. stays ▲ _□_ _ _ _ _
22. horsemen ■ _□_ _ _ _ _

23. convinced ■ _ _ _ _ _ _ _ _□_ _
24. finished ■ _□_ _ _ _ _ _ _ _
25. planning ★ □_ _ _ _ _ _ _ _

26. Proverb: _ _ o _ e   wh _   l _ v _   _ n   _ l _ s _   h _ _ s _ _

_ o   _ o _   _ e _ _   w _ _ _ _ w _ .

administration	concrete	fatal	lieutenant	previous
agency	confined	humane	joyous	publication
ancient	consideration	hygiene	notation	quotation
cereal	contrary	interfere	occasion	society
combination	convene	interior	preside	trifle

C. Symbols and Signs Use the symbols to write Other Word Forms for each spelling word. For some words, you need to add or subtract a letter, or both, before adding the ending. If you need help, use the **Spelling Dictionary**.

☆ = ing   ▲ = es   ■ = ic   ● = s   ◆ = ly

1. fatal ◆ No one was _____ injured by the earthquake.

2. ancient ● This land between the rivers belonged to the _____ .

3. consideration ● We will discuss several _____ .

4. society ▲ Modern _____ are extremely complex.

5. convene ☆ The delegates will be _____ soon.

6. concrete ◆ The problem was presented _____ .

7. interior ● We must paint the _____ of several apartments.

8. preside ☆ The senator is _____ at the meeting.

9. notation ● I made several _____ .

10. trifle ☆ The fee is a _____ cost.

11. hygiene ■ The operating room's equipment has to be very _____ .

12. publication ● We subscribe to three _____ .

13. agency ▲ More insurance _____ now sell fire policies.

14. administration ● The last two _____ in our town have lacked authority.

15. cereal ● Buy several kinds of _____ for our breakfast.

16. occasion ● We met on two _____ .

17. interfere ☆ The children are not _____ with my work.

18. joyous ◆ The fans cheered _____ .

19. lieutenant ● Three _____ met with the major.

20. previous ◆ We were introduced _____ .

21. combination ● Several color _____ were included in the design.

22. confined ☆ This small chair is very _____ .

23. quotation ● The teacher read two _____ from the poem.

24. humane ◆ All animals should be treated _____ .

25. contrary ◆ After I gave the direction, the child behaved _____ .

■ occupation ★ vocation ▲ require ♦ groove ○ acquired
canoe resides mere theory pollution
examination civilization describe bestow automation
create sigh generation youth pursue
sensation limitation aside gracious conclusion

D. Books and Authors

Write Other Word Forms or the spelling words to complete the book titles. The shape tells you in what column you can find the spelling word. Use each word or its Other Word Form only once. Capitalize each word. If you need help, use the **Spelling Dictionary**.

1. The Causes of ★ _____ and Yawning by Ho Hum Lo

2. Facts and ♦ _____ for the Chemist by Bunsen Burner

3. The Homeowner's Repair Manual for ○ _____ Washers by Bea A. Handimann

4. The Worker's Anthology of New ■ _____ by Anita Jobb

5. Basic ▲ _____ for Bird Watching by Bob O. Link

6. The ■ _____ and Presentation of Congressional Speeches by Phil E. Buster

7. For a More ♦ _____ Face by Lynes R. Gonn

8. The Actor's Book of Famous ▲ _____ and Remarks by Ima Seene Steeler

9. Story Writing: Great Plots and ○ _____ by I. Will Finnish

10. The Sport of ■ _____ by Tip N. Sink

11. Friends and Foes in a ★ _____ Society by Warren Peace

12. Hello, World! It's ▲ _____ Me! by U. R. Needed

13. The ○ _____ of Truth by Frank N. Candid

14. The Sky's the ★ _____ by A. V. Ashun

15. How to Behave ♦ _____ in Times of Stress by Hugh B. Kalm

16. Careers and ★ _____ by Harr D. Labors

17. Where Nocturnal Animals ★ _____ by Batson Owells

18. The Gifts ♦ _____ by Our Forefathers by Ann Sestor

19. The Writer's Handbook for Improving ▲ _____ by Moore D. Taile

20. Six Ways to ○ _____ Better Reading Skills by Rita Booke

21. The Merger of Younger and Older ▲ _____ by Patience N. Prudence

22. The Rivers We ○ _____ by Derr T. Waters

23. The Importance of Eye ■ _____ by Yul C. Betta

24. Your Mysterious Sixth ■ _____ by Deja Bous

25. Needles, Discs, and ♦ _____ by Fone O. Graff

13

A. Pretest and Proofreading

B. Spelling Words and Phrases

1. **vast** — vast fields
2. **shaft** — a mine shaft
3. **splash** — heard the splash
4. **alley** — parked in the alley
5. **rally** — a political rally
6. **latter** — the former or the latter
7. **ballot** — a voting ballot
8. **mammal** — mammal or reptile
9. **grammar** — lesson in grammar
10. **anchor** — a ship's anchor
11. **abstract** — an abstract idea
12. **absolute** — absolute power
13. **rather** — rather late
14. **fashion** — the newest fashion
15. **banquet** — an awards banquet
16. **pageant** — pageant judges
17. **planet** — distant planet
18. **plaster** — ceiling plaster
19. **fracture** — a skull fracture
20. **fragrant** — fragrant aroma

C. Challenge Words and Phrases

1. **alphabetical** — alphabetical order
2. **adjectives** — precise adjectives
3. **fascinated** — fascinated by the moon
4. **fractional** — a fractional part
5. **apparatus** — fire-fighting apparatus

Other Word Forms

vastly, vastness
shafts
splashes, splashed, splashing
alleys
rallies, rallied, rallying
late
ballots, balloted
mammals
grammatical, grammatically
anchored
abstractness
absolutely
fashions, fashionable
banquets
pageants, pageantry
planetary
plastering
fractured
fragrance, fragrantly

D. Scrambled Words Unscramble the scrambled word to find the spelling word that completes the sentence. Write the word.

1. The pep _____ (yallr) was held in the high-school gym.
2. The _____ (ctbastra) painting was on display at the museum.
3. The school held a _____ (ntegapa) to celebrate Independence Day.
4. Good _____ (magrmar) is important for clear communication.
5. The restaurant served chicken at the annual sports _____ (quanbte).
6. The voting _____ (tolbal) had six names on it.
7. The captain threw the _____ (rancoh) from the bow of the boat.
8. We had to park in a narrow _____ (leyal).
9. It took 12 hours for the _____ (aplster) to dry.
10. They dived into the swimming pool with a _____ (shaspl).
11. I will do that in my own _____ (aifonsh).
12. The whale is a sea _____ (lamamm).
13. The explosion caused a large _____ (actefrur) in the wall.
14. The mining _____ (aftsh) was closed due to a landslide.
15. The flower had a _____ (agrfrant) odor.
16. That king ruled with _____ (tubaseol) power.
17. Today we're studying the _____ (tanple) Saturn.
18. A _____ (astv) expanse of ocean lay before us.
19. I would _____ (rarthe) be here than at home.
20. The news came during the _____ (rattle) part of the day.

Spelling Words

vast	shaft	splash	alley	rally	latter	ballot
mammal	grammar	anchor	abstract	absolute		
rather	fashion	banquet	pageant	planet		
plaster	fracture	fragrant				

E. Words and Meanings Write a spelling word for each meaning. Then read down each column to find three more spelling words.

1. a feast ☐ _ _ _ _ _ _

2. a whale _ _ _ _ ☐ _

3. a large meeting _ _ _ ☐ _

4. a narrow street _ ☐ _ _ _

5. a weight that keeps boats in place _ _ _ _ ☐ _

6. hard to understand _ _ _ ☐ _ _ _

7. a special play ☐ _ _ _ _ _ _

8. a mixture of lime, sand, and water _ ☐ _ _ _ _ _

9. a dash of water _ _ _ ☐ _ _

10. pleasant smelling _ _ _ _ _ _ ☐ _

11. total _ _ _ _ _ _ _ ☐

12. not the first _ _ ☐ _ _ _

13. great in area _ _ ☐ _

14. style _ _ _ ☐ _ _ _

15. the rules of a language _ _ ☐ _ _ _ _

16. a crack or break ☐ _ _ _ _ _ _ _

17. somewhat _ _ ☐ _ _ _

18. Write the three spelling words made by the sets of boxes.

F. Using Other Word Forms Write the Other Word Form that fits each clue.

   1. being a celestial body _____ (planet)
   2. big meetings _____ (rally)
   3. greatly _____ (vast)
   4. according to the rules of language _____ (grammar)
   5. without a doubt _____ (absolute)

G. Challenge Words Write the Challenge Word that completes each phrase or sentence.

alphabetical	adjectives	fascinated	fractional	apparatus

   1. in _____ order
   2. Descriptive words are called _____ .
   3. enchanted or _____ by the sight
   4. a small or _____ part of the group
   5. weight-lifting equipment or _____

H. Spelling and Writing Write two or more questions about each statement. Use as many Spelling Words, Other Word Forms, and Challenge Words as you can. A few words are suggested. Proofread for spelling using one of the Proofreading Tips from the Yellow Pages.

   1. Watching whales can be an awesome adventure.
      mammal   anchor   planet   vast   splash   absolutely   fascinated

      Example: How do scientists find the <u>absolute</u> spot to see these huge <u>mammals</u> in the <u>vast</u> ocean?

   2. The city planned a great celebration to mark its one hundredth anniversary.
      banquet   pageant   fashion   rally   alley   grammar   apparatus

   3. Each student voted on the decoration of the school lobby.
      ballot   plaster   fracture   abstract   rather   shaft   alphabetical

14

A. Pretest and Proofreading

B. Spelling Words and Phrases

1. **edit**   will edit the story
2. **theft**   charged with theft
3. **scent**   lost the scent
4. **sketch**   a sketch pad
5. **medal**   awarded a medal
6. **render**   will render it useless
7. **splendor**   dawn's splendor
8. **cemetery**   local cemetery
9. **secretary**   a skilled secretary
10. **generally**   is generally on time
11. **residence**   a new residence
12. **decorator**   interior decorator
13. **centimeter**   one centimeter long
14. **legislature**   elected to the legislature
15. **helicopter**   helicopter pilot
16. **develop**   to develop an idea
17. **perfectly**   perfectly made
18. **unexpected**   an unexpected guest
19. **intelligent**   an intelligent answer
20. **investigate**   to investigate crimes

C. Challenge Words and Phrases

1. **spectrum**   a star's spectrum
2. **investment**   the wise investment
3. **specialized**   specialized tools
4. **electronic**   some electronic games
5. **spectacular**   a spectacular view

Other Word Forms

edited, editor, editorial
thief, thieves, thefts
scented
sketches, sketching
medals
rendered
splendid
cemeteries
secretaries
general, generalize
reside, residential
decorate
centimeters
legislate
helicopters
developed, developing
perfect, perfection
expect, unexpectedly
intelligence
investigating, investigation

D. Word Search The spelling words can be found in the word puzzle. The words appear across, down, and diagonally. Write the words.

Across

1.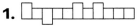

2.

3.

4.

5.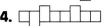

6.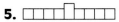

7.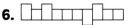

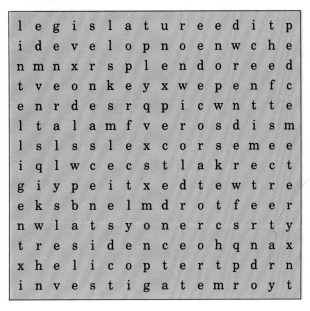

l	e	g	i	s	l	a	t	u	r	e	e	d	i	t	p
i	d	e	v	e	l	o	p	n	o	e	n	w	c	h	e
n	m	n	x	r	s	p	l	e	n	d	o	r	e	e	d
t	v	e	o	n	k	e	y	x	w	e	p	e	n	f	c
e	n	r	d	e	s	r	q	p	i	c	w	n	t	t	e
l	t	a	l	a	m	f	v	e	r	o	s	d	i	s	m
l	s	l	s	s	l	e	x	c	o	r	s	e	m	e	e
i	q	l	w	c	e	c	s	t	l	a	k	r	e	c	t
g	i	y	p	e	i	t	x	e	d	t	e	w	t	r	e
e	k	s	b	n	e	l	m	d	r	o	t	f	e	e	r
n	w	l	a	t	s	y	o	n	e	r	c	s	r	t	y
t	r	e	s	i	d	e	n	c	e	o	h	q	n	a	x
x	h	e	l	i	c	o	p	t	e	r	t	p	d	r	n
i	n	v	e	s	t	i	g	a	t	e	m	r	o	y	t

Down

8.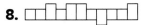

9.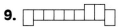

10.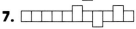

11.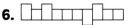

12.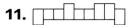

13.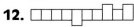

14.

15.

16.

17.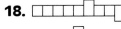

18.

19.

Diagonally

20.

E. Sort Your Words In alphabetical order, write the spelling words under the correct headings.

Words with One Syllable	Words with Three Syllables	Words with Four Syllables
1. ____ 3. ____	8. ____ 10. ____	11. ____ 16. ____
2. ____	9. ____	12. ____ 17. ____
		13. ____ 18. ____
Words with Two Syllables		14. ____ 19. ____
4. ____ 6. ____		15. ____ 20. ____
5. ____ 7. ____		

Spelling Words

edit   theft   scent   sketch   medal   render   splendor
cemetery   secretary   generally   residence   decorator
centimeter   legislature   helicopter   develop   perfectly
unexpected   intelligent   investigate

F. Crossword Puzzle Solve the puzzle by writing all the words from the spelling list. Check your answers in the **Spelling Dictionary**.

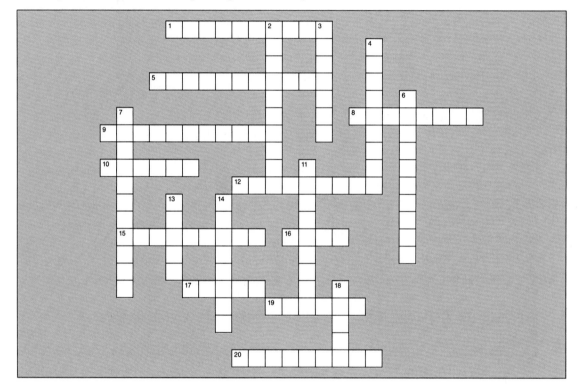

Across

1. not planned on
5. a lawmaking group
8. a burial ground
9. to search carefully
10. to cause to become
12. faultlessly
15. usually
16. to correct errors in writing
17. a badge of honor
19. to draw
20. a person who decorates

Down

2. a measurement
3. to grow
4. an office worker
6. an air vehicle
7. smart
11. one's home
13. the act of stealing
14. glory
18. an odor

G. Using Other Word Forms Write the Other Word Form that completes each sentence.

1. He used his mental ability. It was his _____ (intelligent) that helped solve the problem.
2. She wrote her opinion as editor of the paper. The article was a strong _____ (edit).
3. She was a good office worker. She was one of the best _____ (secretary).
4. The detective searched the scene of the crime. He began his _____ (investigate).
5. First he will list all the parts. Then he will _____ (generally) about them and give us his conclusion.

H. Challenge Words Write the Challenge Word that completes each question.

spectrum	investment	specialized	electronic	spectacular

1. Is an _____ appliance dangerous to use during a thunderstorm?
2. How many doctors _____ in treating cancer?
3. What are the different colors of the _____ ?
4. Was the eclipse of the moon a wonderful, _____ event?
5. Does your hobby require a large _____ of the time and money?

I. Spelling and Writing Write *two* or more answers to each question. Use as many Spelling Words, Other Word Forms, and Challenge Words as you can. A few words are suggested. Proofread your work.

1. If you were a great inventor, what might you create for your next invention?
   sketch – helicopter – develop – electronic – spectacular – centimeter

2. How would you respond if a famous detective asked you for help in solving a baffling case?
   render – theft – unexpected – investigate – intelligent – perfectly

3. If you were an interior decorator, what might you write as an advertisement in a newspaper?
   spectrum – medal – splendor – decorator – residence – specialized

15

A. Pretest and Proofreading

B. Spelling Words and Phrases

1. **grim**   a grim tale
2. **skidded**   skidded on the ice
3. **hitched**   hitched up the horses
4. **hinge**   squeaky hinge
5. **glimpse**   a glimpse inside
6. **insulted**   insulted the guests
7. **instance**   in every instance
8. **inhabitant**   a city inhabitant
9. **disturbance**   a loud disturbance
10. **disagreeable**   one disagreeable tourist
11. **victim**   a tornado victim
12. **witness**   the only witness
13. **wither**   to fade and wither
14. **whimper**   heard a whimper
15. **whispered**   whispered to me
16. **kindling**   wood for kindling
17. **biscuit**   a fresh biscuit
18. **mischief**   very little mischief
19. **brilliant**   brilliant color
20. **privilege**   a special privilege

C. Challenge Words and Phrases

1. **caterpillar**   a banded caterpillar
2. **exquisite**   the exquisite painting
3. **prehistoric**   prehistoric life
4. **restricted**   restricted parking
5. **possessive**   a possessive pronoun

Other Word Forms

grimmer, grimmest, grimly
skid, skidding
hitch, hitches, hitching
hinges
glimpsed, glimpsing
insult, insults, insulting
instant, instances,
  instantaneous
inhabit
disturb, disturbed
disagree, disagreeing
victimize
witnesses
withered
whimpering
whisper
kindle, kindles, kindled
biscuits
mischievous
brilliance, brilliantly
privileges

D. Rhyme Time

Write the spelling word that rhymes with each of the words below.

1. distance
2. trim
3. limper
4. switched
5. knit
6. kidded

7. limps
8. fitness
9. dwindling
10. dither
11. resulted
12. twinge

Write the eight words that did not rhyme with any of the words above.

E. All in a Row

Write the twenty spelling words in alphabetical order. Then join the boxed letters and write four hidden words.

1. _ _ □ _ _ _ _
2. _ _ _ _ _ _ _ □
3. _ _ _ □ □ _ _ _ _ _ _
4. _ □ _ _ _ _ _ _ □ _ _
5. □ _ _ _ _ _ _
6. Hidden Word: _____

7. _ _ _ □
8. _ _ _ _ □
9. _ _ _ _ _ _ □
10. □ _ _ _ _ _ _ □ _ _
11. _ _ _ _ _ □ _ _
12. Hidden Word: _____

13. _ _ □ _ _ _ _ _
14. _ _ _ _ _ □ _ _
15. □ _ _ _ _ _ _ _
16. □ _ _ _ _ □ _ _ _
17. _ _ _ _ _ _ □ _
18. Hidden Word: _____

19. _ _ □ _ _ _
20. _ □ _ _ _ □ _
21. _ _ _ _ _ □ _ _ _
22. _ _ _ _ _ _ □
23. _ _ _ _ _ _ _ □
24. Hidden Word: _____

Spelling Words

grim skidded hitched hinge glimpse insulted instance inhabitant disturbance disagreeable victim witness wither whimper whispered kindling biscuit mischief brilliant privilege

F. Bases and Suffixes The spelling list contains twelve base words and eight words with suffixes. Write each spelling word.

Words with Suffixes	Base Words	Words with Suffixes	Base Words
1. grimly	_____	11. brilliantly	_____
2. instances	_____	12. witnesses	_____
3. glimpsed	_____	13. _____	kindle
4. whimpering	_____	14. _____	inhabit
5. biscuits	_____	15. _____	whisper
6. victimize	_____	16. _____	insult
7. hinges	_____	17. _____	skid
8. mischievous	_____	18. _____	hitch
9. privileges	_____	19. _____	disagree
10. withered	_____	20. _____	disturb

G. Complete the Equations Write the spelling words to complete the equations. The sign ≠ means "does not equal." If you need help, use the **Spelling Dictionary**.

1. attacker ≠
2. gloomy =
3. resident =
4. praised ≠
5. a special right =
6. dull ≠
7. bread roll =
8. dry out =
9. courteous ≠
10. loud moan ≠
11. loud noise =
12. stare ≠
13. sticks of wood =
14. door joint =
15. serious task ≠
16. observer =
17. slipped =
18. shouted ≠
19. moment =
20. untied ≠

H. Using Other Word Forms Write the Other Word Form that completes each sentence.

1. The _____ (grim) character in the tale is the ugly troll.
2. A flash flood will _____ (victim) anyone in its path.
3. Our dog is always digging up our flowers. He is so _____ (mischief).
4. She swept up the child in an _____ (instance) show of emotion.
5. The diamond's _____ (brilliant) was dazzling.

I. Challenge Words Write the Challenge Word that fits each group of words.

caterpillar	exquisite	prehistoric	restricted	possessive

1. old, cave men, mammoths, _____
2. moth, larva, cocoon, _____
3. fenced, guarded, no trespassing, _____
4. noun, pronoun, shows ownership, _____
5. elegant, beautiful, rare, _____

J. Spelling and Writing Write each set of words in a sentence. You may use Other Word Forms. Proofread your work.

1. whimper – victim – whispered
2. instance – glimpse – inhabitant
3. disturbance – insulted – mischief
4. skidded – witness – biscuit
5. disagreeable – privilege – grim
6. wither – kindling – brilliant
7. hitched – hinge – exquisite
8. caterpillar – prehistoric – witnesses
9. restricted – possessive – privileges

16

A. Pretest and Proofreading

B. Spelling Words and Phrases

1. **prompt**   <u>prompt</u> service
2. **motto**   the state <u>motto</u>
3. **hobbies**   games or <u>hobbies</u>
4. **comet**   tail of the <u>comet</u>
5. **copied**   <u>copied</u> over again
6. **conquer**   to <u>conquer</u> the wilderness
7. **contact**   finally made <u>contact</u>
8. **constant**   <u>constant</u> motion
9. **column**   <u>column</u> or row
10. **solid**   a <u>solid</u> mass
11. **monstrous**   a <u>monstrous</u> task
12. **process**   the legal <u>process</u>
13. **progress**   making <u>progress</u>
14. **nonsense**   to talk <u>nonsense</u>
15. **apologize**   should <u>apologize</u>
16. **economy**   a strong <u>economy</u>
17. **democracy**   formed a <u>democracy</u>
18. **geography**   local <u>geography</u>
19. **thermometer**   had read the <u>thermometer</u>
20. **carbon**   a <u>carbon</u> copy

Other Word Forms

promptly, promptness
mottos
hobby
comets
copy, copying, copier
conquered, conquering
contacted
constantly
columned, columnist
solidify, solidifies
monster
processes, processing
progressed, progression,
   progressive
nonsensical
apology, apologies,
   apologized
economies, economical
democracies, democratic
geographies, geographic
thermometers
carbons

C. Challenge Words and Phrases

1. **allotted**   in the <u>allotted</u> time
2. **apostrophe**   with an <u>apostrophe</u>
3. **component**   every needed <u>component</u>
4. **longitude**   latitude and <u>longitude</u>
5. **consonant**   the beginning <u>consonant</u>

D. Break the Code Use the code to write the spelling words.

a	b	c	d	e	f	g	h	i	j	k	l	m	n	o	p	q	r	s	t	u	v	w	x	y	z
↓	↓	↓	↓	↓	↓	↓	↓	↓	↓	↓	↓	↓	↓	↓	↓	↓	↓	↓	↓	↓	↓	↓	↓	↓	↓
f	e	o	p	x	v	a	s	j	k	w	n	t	g	u	l	z	q	c	r	m	d	y	h	i	b

1. dtcudm

2. sgtzcl

3. sclmgsm

4. hcpyv

5. bsclcuw

6. scdybv

7. scpoul

8. ucmmc

9. dtcsbhh

10. scubm

11. xczzybh

12. vbucstgsw

13. nbcntgdxw

14. uclhmtcoh

15. sclrobt

16. dtcntbhh

17. lclhblhb

18. sclhmglm

19. gdcpcnyqb

20. mxbtucubmbt

E. Sort Your *O*'s Write each spelling word under the correct headings. A word may go under more than one heading.

Letter *o* in the First or Only Syllable

1. ____   **8.** ____

2. ____   **9.** ____

3. ____   **10.** ____

4. ____   **11.** ____

5. ____   **12.** ____

6. ____   **13.** ____

7. ____   **14.** ____

Letter *o* in the Second Syllable

15. ____   **19.** ____

16. ____   **20.** ____

17. ____   **21.** ____

18. ____   **22.** ____

Letter *o* in the Third Syllable

23. ____   **24.** ____

Spelling Words

prompt motto hobbies comet copied conquer
contact constant column solid monstrous
process progress nonsense apologize economy
democracy geography thermometer carbon

F. Hidden Words The spelling words and some Other Word Forms (p. 64) can be found in the grid below. The words appear across, down, and diagonally. Write the words.

Spelling Words

Across

1.
2.
3.
4.
5.
6.
7.
8.
9.
10.
11.
12.

```
t h e r m o m e t e r m o t t o
d a g n o n s e n s e z r l d c
e b e u n a p o l o g i z e p o
m c o n s t a n t l y m j c l p
o o g d t t s o l i d o l o g y
c n r c r c o l u m n p k n m p
r q a c o p i e d c a r b o n r
a u p o u m m x b d y o r m q o
c e h r s t e r l l z c u y z m
y r y p c o n t a c t e x l o p
c z l x w p r o g r e s s e d t
h o b b i e s l i z p s q u u d
v p r o g r e s s m o t t o s t
t c o n s t a n t m o n s t e r
```

Down

13.
14.
15.
16.
17.
18.
19.

Diagonally

20.

Other Word Forms

Across

21.
22.
23.
24.

Down

25.

G. Using Other Word Forms
Add an ending to each noun to make it an adjective. Then write this Other Word Form to complete each phrase.

Noun	Adjective
1. nonsense	your ___ behavior
2. economy	an ___ fuel
3. democracy	a ___ convention
4. geography	the ___ location
5. progress	a ___ idea

H. Challenge Words
Write the Challenge Word that completes each sentence.

allotted	apostrophe	component	longitude	consonant

1. Speakers are an important ___ of a stereo system.

2. The letter **a** is a vowel and **b** is a ___ .

3. The omitted letter in a contraction is indicated by an ___ .

4. We ___ two thousand dollars for future vacations.

5. Lines of latitude and ___ pinpoint the location.

I. Spelling and Writing
Write two or more answers to each question. Use as many Spelling Words, Other Word Forms, and Challenge Words as you can. A few words are suggested. Proofread for spelling using one of the Proofreading Tips from the Yellow Pages.

1. Why might the space aliens come to our planet?
nonsense   democracy   economy   conquer   contact   monstrous

2. How should teachers present information?
progress   solid   geography   constant   prompt   apologize

3. How will the mad scientist proceed with the experiment?
carbon   process   column   thermometer   copied   comet

17

A. Pretest and Proofreading

B. Spelling Words and Phrases

1. **usher** — followed the <u>usher</u>
2. **utter** — <u>utter</u> confusion
3. **utmost** — tried their <u>utmost</u>
4. **underdog** — cheered the <u>underdog</u>
5. **numb** — <u>numb</u> with cold
6. **bluffed** — <u>bluffed</u> my way
7. **bumper** — dented the <u>bumper</u>
8. **slumber** — a deep <u>slumber</u>
9. **custom** — unusual <u>custom</u>
10. **accustomed** — not <u>accustomed</u> to waiting
11. **mustard** — <u>mustard</u> or ketchup
12. **justice** — to seek <u>justice</u>
13. **substance** — a smooth <u>substance</u>
14. **substitute** — <u>substitute</u> teacher
15. **summon** — to <u>summon</u> to court
16. **puzzling** — a <u>puzzling</u> situation
17. **luncheon** — a <u>luncheon</u> menu
18. **luxury** — necessity or <u>luxury</u>
19. **consult** — to <u>consult</u> an expert
20. **production** — <u>production</u> crew

Other Word Forms

ushering
uttered, utterance, uttermost
underdogs
numbs, numbness
bluff
bump, bumping
slumbered
customize, customary, accustom
mustards
just, justify
substantial
substituted, substitution
summons, summoned, summonses
puzzle, puzzled
lunch, luncheons
luxuries
consultant
produce, product

C. Challenge Words and Phrases

1. **constructive** — a <u>constructive</u> comment
2. **unfamiliar** — <u>unfamiliar</u> faces
3. **fundamental** — the <u>fundamental</u> idea
4. **productive** — a <u>productive</u> morning
5. **muscular** — <u>muscular</u> development

D. Sort Your Words In alphabetical order, write the spelling words under the correct headings.

Words with One Syllable		Words with Two Syllables		Words with Three Syllables	
1. ____	2. ____	3. ____	10. ____	16. ____	19. ____
		4. ____	11. ____	17. ____	20. ____
		5. ____	12. ____	18. ____	
		6. ____	13. ____		
		7. ____	14. ____		
		8. ____	15. ____		
		9. ____			

E. Scrambled Words Unscramble each scrambled word to find a word from the spelling list. Write the words.

1. bunm
2. trute
3. stomut
4. ruluxy
5. gonudder
6. csonltu
7. juciest
8. unmmos
9. canbusest
10. stomuc
11. ermbusl
12. bistettusu
13. inctoprodu
14. chennulo
15. umpebr
16. ustrdma
17. zpuzngil
18. shuer
19. accstumode
20. ffublde

Working Words in Spelling **69**

Spelling Words

usher	utter	utmost	underdog	numb	bluffed
bumper	slumber	custom	accustomed	mustard	
justice	substance	substitute	summon	puzzling	
luncheon	luxury	consult	production		

F. Cause and Effect Write a word from the spelling list to complete each sentence.

1. If a person is helping you down the aisle, he or she is probably an _____ .

2. If your teacher is absent, you have a _____ .

3. If you are used to your old sneakers, you are _____ to them.

4. If you call to your dog, you _____ her.

5. If you are eating a meal at noon, you could be at a _____ .

6. If everyone believes your tall tale, you have _____ successfully.

7. If you are not likely to win the game, you are the _____ .

8. If you own more than you need, you probably live in _____ .

9. If the factory is very busy, its _____ is high.

10. If you cannot figure out the answer, the problem is _____ .

11. If you have been treated fairly, you feel you have received _____ .

12. If you are fast asleep, you are deep in _____ .

13. If you hit the outside front or back rim of a car, you have hit the _____ .

14. If you put a yellow sauce on your hot dog, you are using _____ .

15. If you slipped on the floor, you probably stepped on a greasy _____ .

16. If you celebrate a holiday, you are following a _____ .

17. If you have been sent to the farthest place, you are at the _____ point.

18. If you say something out loud, you _____ it.

19. If you have no feeling in your hand, your hand may be _____ .

20. If you have a conference with your teachers, you probably will _____ with them.

G. Using Other Word Forms Write the Other Word Form that fits each clue.

1. person who provides expert advice _____ (consult)
2. is usual _____ (custom)
3. written warnings to appear in court _____ (summon)
4. to support with a good reason _____ (justice)
5. large or important _____ (substance)

H. Challenge Words Write the Challenge Word that completes each sentence.

constructive	unfamiliar	fundamental	productive	muscular

1. If the author is not know, she may be _____ .
2. If a person lifts weights, she may become _____ .
3. If it is a basic skill, it is _____ .
4. If the criticism is helpful, it is _____ .
5. If the student is a hard worker, he may be _____ .

I. Spelling and Writing Write two or more questions about each statement. Use as many Spelling Words, Other Word Forms, and Challenge Words as you can. A few words are suggested. Proofread for spelling using one of the Proofreading Tips from the Yellow Pages.

1. It is fun to plan a party with a theme.
   luncheon   slumber   consult   production   mustard
      unfamiliar   customary

   Example: Will the <u>customary</u> <u>slumber</u> party have a surprise guest?

2. Many people like science-fiction movies best.
   accustomed   underdog   substances   puzzling   justice   usher
      summon   fundamental

3. Traffic accidents often happen during rainy weather.
   bumper   bluffed   substitute   luxury   utmost   numb
      uttered   constructive

18

■ perfectly	★ luncheon	▲ banquet	◆ mammal	○ sketch
fracture	prompt	fashion	fragrant	residence
decorator	substitute	whispered	splash	develop
ballot	insulted	secretary	scent	unexpected
rally	legislature	theft	inhabitant	helicopter

A. The Things People Do Write Other Word Forms of the spelling words above to complete these sentences about people. If you need help, use the **Spelling Dictionary**.

1. A doctor treats arm ■ ____ .

2. An excellent student looks for a ■ ____ score.

3. A host often ■ ____ a party room.

4. Race-car drivers enjoy car ■ ____ .

5. Voters cast ■ ____ .

6. Senators ★ ____ laws.

7. Punctual people arrive ★ ____ .

8. A rude person might ★ ____ you.

9. Absent teachers require ★ ____ , in the classrooms.

10. Guest speakers attend many ★ ____ .

11. Designers create new ▲ ____ .

12. Club members attend ▲ ____ each year.

13. Office workers may be graduates of ▲ ____ schools.

14. Soft speakers sometimes ▲ ____ .

15. A burglar is also a ▲ ____ .

16. Eskimos ◆ ____ colder regions.

17. Elephants and whales are considered ◆ ____ .

18. Good divers do very little ◆ ____ .

19. Perfume makers want to create a popular ◆ ____ .

20. Bakers can fill a room with wondrous ◆ ____ .

21. The owner may also be a ○ ____ of the house.

22. Photographers are experts in ○ ____ film.

23. Artists sometimes draw ○ ____ .

24. Pilots fly ○ ____ .

25. Magicians can produce coins found ○ ____ behind your ears.

R
E
V
I
E
W

■ alley	★ hitched	▲ brilliant	◆ constant	○ accustomed
anchor	wither	privilege	apologize	mustard
planet	whimper	hobbies	thermometer	justice
cemetery	solid	copied	bluffed	substance
centimeter	biscuit	contact	bumper	production

B. Sentence Completion Write Other Word Forms or the spelling words to complete the sentences. If you need help, use the **Spelling Dictionary**.

1. Narrow passageways between buildings are ■ _____ .
2. Some people like to put ○ _____ on sandwiches.
3. Metal bars attached to cars are ◆ _____ .
4. Stamp collecting is a ▲ _____ you might enjoy.
5. What are the two largest ■ _____ in the solar system?
6. You may hear ★ _____ from an injured dog.
7. Diamonds show their ▲ _____ in direct sunlight.
8. Some speakers can ◆ _____ their way through any discussion.
9. New programs are ○ _____ for television every year.
10. We can measure in ■ _____ or in inches.
11. Strawberries and ★ _____ make a delicious dessert.
12. I will try ▲ _____ the paper over again.
13. Instruments that measure temperature are ◆ _____ .
14. Many ○ _____ change form when heated.
15. The flowers ★ _____ from the lack of rain.
16. By working hard, one may be awarded many ▲ _____ .
17. Burial places are ■ _____ .
18. We are ★ _____ the horses to the wagon for the hayride.
19. If you are ◆ _____ in pain, you should see a doctor.
20. You must ○ _____ yourself to the change in climate.
21. The sailors ■ _____ the ship near the island.
22. In science class, we learned about ★ _____ , liquids, and gases.
23. The police were ▲ _____ when the alarm sounded.
24. The students ◆ _____ to the teacher for being too noisy.
25. I felt the jury was ○ _____ in its decision.

absolute	disagreeable	investigate	nonsense	splendor
column	edit	luxury	pageant	utter
conquer	geography	medal	progress	vast
custom	grammar	mischief	rather	victim
democracy	intelligent	monstrous	render	witness

C. Word Operations Write Other Word Forms for all but one spelling word by performing the operations. If you need help, use the **Spelling Dictionary**.

1. vast + ness =
2. luxury − y + i + ous =
3. victim + ize =
4. render + ing =
5. progress + ion =
6. intelligent + ly =
7. monstrous − us + s + ity =
8. witness + ed =
9. disagreeable − able + ing =
10. medal + ist =
11. nonsense − e + ical =
12. column + ist =
13. custom + ary =
14. geography − y + ic =
15. edit + ion =
16. grammar + ian =
17. mischief − f + v + ous =
18. absolute + ly =
19. conquer + or =
20. democracy − cy + tic =
21. utter + ly =
22. investigate − e + or =
23. splendor − or + id =
24. pageant + ry =

25. Write the spelling word that has no Other Word Form.

R
E
V
I
E
W

abstract	economy	instance	plaster	slumber
carbon	generally	kindling	process	summon
comet	glimpse	latter	puzzling	underdog
consult	grim	motto	shaft	usher
disturbance	hinge	numb	skidded	utmost

D. Word Search Twenty-five Other Word Forms of the spelling words can be found in the word puzzle. The words appear across, down, and diagonally. Write the words. If you need help, use the **Spelling Dictionary**.

Across

1.
2.
3.
4.
5.
6.
7.
8.

Down

9.
10.
11.
12.
13.
14.

15.
16.

Diagonally

17.
18.
19.

20.
21.
22.

23.
24.
25.

```
g t a b s t r a c t n e s s u
e y p l a s t e r e d g l i n
n s k i d s u t t e r l u n d
e x p b m w e m o d f i m s e
r c a r b o n s m v z m b t r
a g o h o j t u q o w p e a d
l b d n f c g t m k n s r n o
i a g i o v e w o b o e e t g
z s t r s m c s t s s s d l s
e h k t i t i u s h e r s y c
p a i i e m u c q e h j z l o
r f n n t r l r a t d r f u m
i t d a g s l y b l i p t z e
m s l m n e o y p u z z l e t
t d e v f g d c o n s u l t s
```

A. Pretest and Proofreading

B. Spelling Words and Phrases

1. ambulance	to call an <u>ambulance</u>
2. analyze	will <u>analyze</u> the results
3. ancestor	an <u>ancestor</u> of mine
4. annual	<u>annual</u> meeting
5. animated	an <u>animated</u> character
6. accurate	<u>accurate</u> time
7. appetite	healthy <u>appetite</u>
8. attitude	a cheerful <u>attitude</u>
9. mansion	a magnificent <u>mansion</u>
10. manager	the team's <u>manager</u>
11. banister	polished the <u>banister</u>
12. candidate	<u>candidate</u> for mayor
13. graduate	a college <u>graduate</u>
14. gallery	an art <u>gallery</u>
15. salary	a weekly <u>salary</u>
16. classify	will <u>classify</u> the data
17. castaway	island <u>castaway</u>
18. parallel	<u>parallel</u> lines
19. blanketed	<u>blanketed</u> with frost
20. adapted	<u>adapted</u> to the cold

C. Challenge Words and Phrases

1. calculate	<u>calculate</u> the cost
2. rectangle	the shape of a <u>rectangle</u>
3. satire	a biting <u>satire</u>
4. aggravate	try not to <u>aggravate</u>
5. raccoons	family of <u>raccoons</u>

Other Word Forms

ambulances
analyzed, analysis
ancestors, ancestral
annually
animate, animating
accurately
appetites
attitudes
mansions
manage, management
banisters
candidates
grade, graduates,
   graduating, graduation
galleries
salaries, salaried
classified, classifying
castaways
paralleled
blanket
adapt, adapts, adapting

D. Break the Code Use the code to write the spelling words.

a	b	c	d	e	f	g	h	i	j	k	l	m	n	o	p	q	r	s	t	u	v	w	x	y	z
↓	↓	↓	↓	↓	↓	↓	↓	↓	↓	↓	↓	↓	↓	↓	↓	↓	↓	↓	↓	↓	↓	↓	↓	↓	↓
s	p	i	b	d	o	m	u	y	a	r	e	x	j	c	t	g	k	f	n	q	w	z	l	v	h

1. jtcgjple
2. jtolapfk
3. jtthjx
4. qjxxlki
5. djtcaplk
6. ojtecejpl
7. joohkjpl
8. oxjaacsi
9. bjkjxxlx
10. ajxjki

11. jgdhxjtol
12. jppcphel
13. jbblpcpl
14. gjtacft
15. ojapjvji
16. jtjxiwl
17. qkjehjpl
18. jejbple
19. dxjtrlple
20. gjtjqlk

E. Be a Word Detective Find the missing vowels and write the spelling words.

1. __ mb __ l __ nc __
2. m __ ns __ __ n
3. __ d __ pt __ d
4. m __ n __ g __ r
5. c __ nd __ d __ t __
6. __ cc __ r __ t __
7. b __ n __ st __ r
8. c __ st __ w __ __
9. __ nn __ __ l
10. gr __ d __ __ t __

11. p __ r __ ll __ l
12. s __ l __ r __
13. bl __ nk __ t __ d
14. __ n __ l __ z __
15. __ tt __ t __ d __
16. __ nc __ st __ r
17. __ pp __ t __ t __
18. g __ ll __ r __
19. cl __ ss __ f __
20. __ n __ m __ t __ d

Spelling Words

ambulance	analyze	ancestor	annual	animated
accurate	appetite	attitude	mansion	manager
banister	candidate	graduate	gallery	salary
classify	castaway	parallel	blanketed	adapted

F. Words and Meanings Write a spelling word for each meaning. Then read down the column to find one spelling word and one Other Word Form (p. 76).

1. a store supervisor

2. a large house

3. covered

4. precise

5. side-by-side

6. wages

7. created cartoons

8. a shipwrecked person

9. a forefather

10. an area for displaying art

11. a stairway's handrail

12. to study carefully

13. a way of feeling

14. yearly

15. a campaigner

16. made to fit

17. a hunger or craving

18. to sort into groups

19. Write the spelling word and the Other Word Form made by the sets of boxes.

G. Using Other Word Forms Write the Other Word Form that completes each sentence.

1. Putting items in groups is called _____ (classify).
2. A person on the payroll is a _____ (salary) employee.
3. To study the details and draw a conclusion is to make an _____ (analyze).
4. A ceremony at which a person receives a diploma is called _____ (graduate).
5. A home that has belonged to a family for generations is said to be _____ (ancestor).

H. Challenge Words Write the Challenge Word that fits each group of words.

calculate	rectangle	satire	aggravate	raccoons

1. irritate, provoke, _____
2. ridicule, mockery, _____
3. compute, figure, _____
4. beavers, skunks, _____
5. circle, square, _____

I. Spelling and Writing Use each phrase in a sentence. You may want to use the words in a different order or use Other Word Forms. Proofread for spelling using one of the Proofreading Tips from the Yellow Pages.

1. ambulance driver
2. analyze the problem
3. a famous ancestor
4. an annual event
5. animated movies
6. accurate figures
7. no appetite for food
8. the student's attitude
9. historic mansion
10. sales manager
11. gripped the banister
12. supported the candidate
13. graduate from college
14. a shooting gallery
15. a raise in salary
16. classify the books
17. castaway clothing
18. parked parallel to the curb
19. blanketed with snow
20. adapted to the climate

20

A. Pretest and Proofreading

B. Spelling Words and Phrases

1. levy ✓   will <u>levy</u> another tax
2. levee ✓   fished from the <u>levee</u>
3. essay ✓   wrote an <u>essay</u>
4. effect ✓   had no <u>effect</u>
5. excess ✓   <u>excess</u> profits
6. profess ✓   to <u>profess</u> to know
7. session ✓   still in <u>session</u>
8. pressure ✓   tire <u>pressure</u>
9. venture ✓   business <u>venture</u>
10. remedy ✓   a cold <u>remedy</u>
11. specify ✓   to <u>specify</u> which book
12. specimen ✓   a blood <u>specimen</u>
13. sentiment ✓   sharing your <u>sentiment</u>
14. evidence ✓   <u>evidence</u> of a crime
15. reference ✓   a map for <u>reference</u>
16. negligence ✓   because of <u>negligence</u>
17. invest ✓   to <u>invest</u> your time
18. destiny ✓   changed my <u>destiny</u>
19. estimate ✓   made an <u>estimate</u>
20. delicate ✓   a <u>delicate</u> flower

Other Word Forms

levied, levying
levees
essays
effected, effective
excesses, excessive
professed, profession
sessions
press, pressuring
venturing
remedies
specified
specimens
sentiments, sentimental
evidenced, evidently
referred, referring,
  references
neglect, negligent
investing
destinies
estimating
delicately

C. Challenge Words and Phrases

1. **contented**   feeling very <u>contented</u>
2. **parentheses**   needs <u>parentheses</u>
3. **concentrated**   <u>concentrated</u> on the problem
4. **measurements**   approximate <u>measurements</u>
5. **relentless**   a <u>relentless</u> search

D. What the Dickens! Write the spelling words to solve the puzzle. Read down the column to find the title of a book by Charles Dickens.

1. carelessness   _ _ ☐ _ _ _ _ _ _ _

2. to claim to know   _ ☐ _ _ _ _ _

3. a riverbank   _ ☐ _ _ _

4. a composition   _ _ _ ☐ _

5. fragile   _ _ _ _ _ _ ☐ _

6. a cure   _ _ _ ☐ _ _

7. extra   _ ☐ _ _ _

8. force   ☐ _ _ _ _ _ _ _

9. result   _ _ _ ☐ _ _

10. a sample   _ _ _ ☐ _ _ _

11. a risk   _ _ _ ☐ _ _

12. to guess   _ _ _ _ _ ☐ _

13. emotion or feeling   _ _ _ ☐ _ _ _ _

14. something that gives proof   _ _ ☐ _ _ _ _ _

15. a meeting   _ _ _ _ _ ☐ _

16. to put money into stocks   _ ☐ _ _ _ _

17. fate   _ _ ☐ _ _ _

18. Write the book title.

19. Write the three spelling words not used in the puzzle.

Spelling Words

levy levee essay effect excess profess session pressure venture remedy specify specimen sentiment evidence reference negligence invest destiny estimate delicate	

E. Not _____ , But Write each of the spelling words for one of the phrases.

1. not frail, but _____

2. not a guess, but an _____

3. not to buy stock, but to _____

4. not a composition, but an _____

5. not extra, but _____

6. not a result, but an _____

7. not to point out, but to _____

8. not feeling, but _____

9. not fate, but _____

10. not a riverbank, but a _____

11. not to collect fees, but to _____

12. not a meeting, but a _____

13. not proof, but _____

14. not a risk, but a _____

15. not an information source, but a _____

16. not force, but _____

17. not carelessness, but _____

18. not a sample, but a _____

19. not a cure, but a _____

20. not to pretend, but to _____

F. Using Other Word Forms Write the Other Word Form that completes each series.

1. levies, _____ , levying
2. refer, _____ , referring
3. specifies, _____ , specifying
4. invests, invested, _____
5. estimates, estimated, _____

G. Challenge Words Write the Challenge Word that completes each phrase.

contented	parentheses	concentrated	measurements	relentless

1. dimensions and _____
2. focused and _____
3. satisfied and _____
4. brackets and _____
5. unyielding and _____

H. Spelling and Writing Write each set of words in a sentence. You may use Other Word Forms. Proofread for spelling using one of the Proofreading Tips from the Yellow Pages.

1. venture, levee, specify
2. profess, excess, evidence
3. effect, levy, estimate
4. reference, specimen, delicate
5. essay, invest, remedy
6. destiny, sentiment, effect
7. session, negligence, profess
8. pressure, evidence, estimate
9. specimen, essay, reference

21

A. Pretest and Proofreading

B. Spelling Words and Phrases

1. **entrance** — front entrance
2. **essence** — essence of the idea
3. **escapade** — daring escapade
4. **especially** — especially pleased
5. **execute** — to execute power
6. **celebrate** — will celebrate the holiday
7. **vegetate** — to vegetate in the soil
8. **legislate** — a law to legislate
9. **desperate** — desperate situation
10. **temperate** — temperate climate
11. **senate** — where the senate meets
12. **decade** — a decade ago
13. **precious** — precious gems
14. **federal** — federal building
15. **vessel** — an ocean vessel
16. **wrestle** — wrestle to the ground
17. **representative** — senator or representative
18. **succession** — in quick succession
19. **detour** — a temporary detour
20. **depot** — a train depot

Other Word Forms

enter, entrances
essences, essential
escape, escapades
executed, executive
celebrating
vegetated
legislature
despair, desperation
temper, temperature
senates, senator
decades
preciously
federate
vessels
wrestled, wrestling
represented, representatives
succeed
detours, detoured
depots

C. Challenge Words and Phrases

1. **necessarily** — not necessarily true
2. **chemicals** — unfamiliar chemicals
3. **nevertheless** — was invited, nevertheless
4. **predicate** — a compound predicate
5. **correspondence** — read the correspondence

D. Crossword Puzzle Solve the puzzle by writing all the words from the spelling list. Check your answers in the **Spelling Dictionary**.

Across
1. not local or state, but _____
3. a train station
5. to make laws
6. an adventure
8. an official agent
10. a lawmaking group
13. a ship
15. a doorway
17. to have a party for a special occasion
18. mild or moderate
19. a sequential order

Down
2. hopeless
3. an alternate route
4. ten years
7. valuable
9. particularly
11. the most necessary part
12. not to fight, but to _____
14. to grow in the soil
16. to put into use

Spelling Words

entrance   essence   escapade   especially   execute *celebrate   vegetate   legislate   desperate   temperate* *senate   decade   precious   federal   vessel   wrestle* *representative   succession   detour   depot*

E. Be a Sentence Detective Unscramble the word under each blank. Write each unscrambled word.

1. The _____ will _____ that bill into law.
 asneet   glaeteisl

2. The _____ to the _____ is on the other side of the building.
 traencen   toped

3. To _____ , you must _____ many difficult moves.
 stleewr   eceteux

4. I worked for a _____ as a company _____ .
 addece   preernesatvite

5. This historical _____ was once involved in a thrilling _____ .
 sleves   aadesecp

6. The _____ agents charted a _____ for the presidential motorcade.
 redleaf   routed

7. The _____ of this plan is _____ appealing to me.
 scenese   leylispeac

8. We hope the plants will _____ in such a _____ climate.
 eattevge   ermpteate

9. His _____ to the throne created a _____ situation.
 inosecscus   sedepreta

10. We will _____ your birthday by giving you a _____ jewel.
 ebrcleate   prseicou

F. Using Other Word Forms Write the Other Word Form that completes each sentence.

1. After discussing the issue, the state _____ (legislate) passed the law.

2. They were fighting for the championship. The _____ (wrestle) match was for the gold medal.

3. It is 104 degrees outside. The _____ (temperate) is very high.

4. This spice is _____ (essence) to the recipe; otherwise the soup will be bland.

5. The company president met with the vice presidents. It was an _____ (execute) meeting.

G. Challenge Words Write the Challenge Word that completes each sentence.

necessarily	chemicals	nevertheless	predicate	correspondence

1. Each sentence has a subject and a _____ .

2. I had very little energy; _____ , I continued to work.

3. I found the stationery, so I could continue my _____ .

4. A laboratory technician often works with _____ .

5. Some newspaper reports are not _____ true; sometimes they are based on rumor.

H. Spelling and Writing Write *two* or more answers to each question. Use as many Spelling Words, Other Word Forms, and Challenge Words as you can. A few words are suggested. Proofread your work.

1. What might happen if you tried to ride your racing bike through a construction site?

entrance – nevertheless – escapade – detour – especially

2. What would you do if you wanted to become a champion athlete?

necessarily – decade – execute – precious – wrestle – desperate

3. What would you do to try to change a new national law that you felt was unjust?

federal – senate – legislate – representative – correspondence – essence

22

A. Pretest and Proofreading

B. Spelling Words and Phrases

1. **invisible**   invisible ink
2. **initial**   middle initial
3. **individual**   individual servings
4. **innocent**   innocent or guilty
5. **incident**   a shocking incident
6. **indifferent**   indifferent to change
7. **influence**   a friend's influence
8. **intellect**   great intellect
9. **interview**   a job interview
10. **interval**   a five-minute interval
11. **international**   an international incident
12. **indicate**   will indicate progress
13. **irrigate**   to irrigate the fields
14. **liberate**   will liberate the prisoners
15. **situated**   situated nearby
16. **artificial**   artificial turf
17. **official**   official decision
18. **original**   original manuscript
19. **principle**   matter of principle
20. **miserable**   miserable weather

C. Challenge Words and Phrases

1. **affliction**   a mild affliction
2. **statistics**   recent statistics
3. **evicted**   will not be evicted
4. **bewildered**   bewildered by the comment
5. **peninsula**   a marshy peninsula

Other Word Forms

visible, invisibleness
initialed
individually, individuals
innocently, innocence
incidental, incidence
differ, indifferently
influencing
intellectual, intelligent
interviewing
intervals
internationally
indicated
irrigating
liberation
situate, situation
artificially
office, officially
origin, originate
principles
misery, miserableness

D. All in a Row Write the twenty spelling words in alphabetical order. Then join the boxed letters and write four hidden words.

1. _ _ _ _ _ ☐ _ _ _ _ _

2. _ _ _ _ _ _ ☐ _ _ _

3. _ _ ☐ _ _ _ _ ☐

4. _ _ _ _ _ _ ☐ _ _ _

5. _ _ _ _ _ _ _ ☐☐

6. Hidden Word: ____

7. _ _ ☐ _ _ _ _ _ _

8. _ _ _ _ _ ☐ _

9. _ _ _ _ ☐ _ _ _

10. ☐ _ _ _ _ _ _ _ _

11. _ _ _ _ _ _ _ ☐ _ _ _ _ ☐

12. Hidden Word: ____

13. ☐ _ _ _ _ _ _ _

14. _ ☐ _ _ _ _ _ _ _ _

15. _ _ ☐ _ _ _ _ ☐

16. _ ☐ _ _ _ _ _ _

17. _ _ _ _ _ _ ☐ _

18. Hidden Word: ____

19. _ _ ☐ _ _ _ _ _ _ _

20. _ _ _ _ ☐ _ _ _

21. ☐ _ _ _ _ _ _ _

22. _ _ _ _ _ _ _ ☐ _ _

23. _ _ _ _ _ _ ☐ _

24. Hidden Word: ____

Spelling Words

invisible	initial	individual	innocent	incident
indifferent	influence	intellect	interview	interval
international	indicate	irrigate	liberate	situated
artificial	official	original	principle	miserable

E. Generally Speaking Write each spelling word for the group it best fits.

1. persuade, affect, _____
2. name, letter, _____
3. sad, unhappy, _____
4. happening, occurrence, _____
5. water, flood, _____
6. not guilty, naive, _____
7. new, first, _____
8. uninvolved, neutral, _____
9. authority, referee, _____
10. universal, global, _____

11. free, let go, _____
12. point out, identify, _____
13. intelligence, mind, _____
14. out of sight, unseen, _____
15. one, alone, _____
16. period, pause, _____
17. consultation, meeting, _____
18. fake, unreal _____
19. law, rule, _____
20. located, placed, _____

F. Break the PBQR Use the code to write the spelling words.

a	b	c	d	e	f	g	h	i	j	k	l	m
↕	↕	↕	↕	↕	↕	↕	↕	↕	↕	↕	↕	↕
n	o	p	q	r	s	t	u	v	w	x	y	z

1. veevtngr
2. vagreiny
3. zvfrenoyr
4. vaivfvoyr
5. bssvpvny
6. vaabprag
7. vapvqrag
8. fvghngrq
9. vaqvssrerag
10. bevtvany

11. vagreivrj
12. vagryyrpg
13. cevapvcyr
14. vavgvny
15. negvsvpvny
16. vasyhrapr
17. vaqvpngr
18. yvorengr
19. vaqvivqhny
20. vagreangvbany

G. Using Other Word Forms

Add an ending to each adjective to make an adverb. Write this Other Word Form to complete each phrase.

	Adjective	Adverb
1.	individual	worked _____ on the project
2.	indifferent	watched the game _____
3.	artificial	_____ sweetened
4.	official	announced the result _____
5.	innocent	responded _____ to the question

H. Challenge Words

Write the Challenge Word that completes each quotation.

affliction	statistics	evicted	bewildered	peninsula

1. Geographer: "Changing ocean currents are eroding the _____ ."

2. Landlord: "I have never _____ a tenant from an apartment."

3. Nurse: "With enough bed rest, your _____ will heal."

4. Sportscaster: "With this winning streak, the team's _____ will improve considerably."

5. Astronomer: "I am _____ by what I see in the night sky."

I. Spelling and Writing

Write each set of words in a sentence. You may use Other Word Forms. Proofread your work.

1. official – influence – interview

2. situated – invisible – indicate

3. miserable – indifferent – incident

4. original – innocent – initial

5. individual – liberate – principle

6. international – irrigate – interval

7. intellect – artificial – internationally

8. affliction – origin – bewildered

9. statistics – peninsula – evicted

23

A. Pretest and Proofreading

B. Spelling Words and Phrases

1. occupy — to <u>occupy</u> the room
2. politics — international <u>politics</u>
3. poverty — <u>poverty</u> level
4. probable — <u>probable</u> outcome
5. profiting — is <u>profiting</u> nobody
6. prosperous — <u>prosperous</u> times
7. prominent — a <u>prominent</u> name
8. monument — a bronze <u>monument</u>
9. columnist — weekly <u>columnist</u>
10. conference — an annual <u>conference</u>
11. contractor — plans of the <u>contractor</u>
12. considerably — <u>considerably</u> more important
13. scholarship — earned a <u>scholarship</u>
14. qualify — to <u>qualify</u> for the final race
15. quality — of excellent <u>quality</u>
16. quantity — great <u>quantity</u>
17. haunt — to <u>haunt</u> the house
18. saucer — <u>saucer</u> of milk
19. cautiously — crossed <u>cautiously</u>
20. ought — <u>ought</u> to know

Other Word Forms

occupies, occupied,
    occupying
political, politician
probably, probability
profit
prosper, prospered
prominence, prominently
monumental
columns
confer, conferred, conferring
contract, contracting
consider, considerate
scholar
qualified, qualifying
qualities
quantities
haunted
sauce, saucers
caution, cautious

C. Challenge Words and Phrases

1. crocodile — a hungry <u>crocodile</u>
2. monotonous — a <u>monotonous</u> voice
3. molecule — a <u>molecule</u> of oxygen
4. pentagon — corners of a <u>pentagon</u>
5. responsive — <u>responsive</u> audiences

D. All in a Row Write the twenty spelling words in alphabetical order. Then join the boxed letters and write four hidden words.

1. _ _ _ _ _ _ _☐_ _

2. _ _ _ _ _ _ _ _☐

3. _ _ _ _ _☐_ _ _ _

4. _ _ _ _☐_ _ _ _ _ _

5. ☐_ _ _ _ _ _☐_ _

6. Hidden Word: ____

7. ☐_ _ _ _ _

8. _ _ _ _ _ _☐_ _

9. _ _☐_ _ _

10. _ _ _ _☐_

11. _ _ _☐_ _☐_

12. Hidden Word: ____

13. ☐_ _ _ _ _ _ _

14. _☐_ _ _ _ _ _ _

15. _ _ _ _☐_ _ _ _

16. _ _ _☐_ _ _ _ _

17. _ _ _ _ _☐_ _ _ _

18. Hidden Word: ____

19. _ _ _☐_ _ _ _

20. _ _ _ _ _ _ _☐

21. _ _ _☐_ _ _ _ _

22. _ _ _☐_ _ _

23. _ _☐_ _ _ _ _ _ _ _

24. Hidden Word: ____

E. Guide Words These word pairs are guide words that might appear in a dictionary. Write the words from the spelling list that would appear on the same page as each pair of guide words.

bullpen–circumference
1. ____

civil–compare
2. ____

compete–continue
3. ____ 4. ____

continuous–define
5. ____

harry–incident
6. ____

memorial–neglect
7. ____

negligence–organize
8. ____

origin–please
9. ____

plentiful–proceed
10. ____ 12. ____
11. ____

process–qualify
13. ____ 15. ____
14. ____ 16. ____

quality–remember
17. ____ 18. ____

remembrance–scaling
19. ____

scent–sleigh
20. ____

Spelling Words

occupy   politics   poverty   probable   profiting
prosperous   prominent   monument   columnist
conference   contractor   considerably   scholarship
qualify   quality   quantity   haunt   saucer
cautiously   ought

F. Word Search The spelling words and seven Other Word Forms (p. 92) can be found in the word puzzle. The words appear across, down, and diagonally. Write the words.

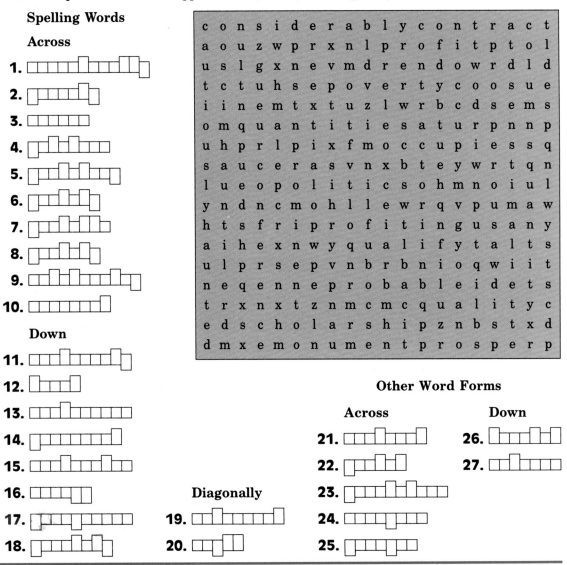

Spelling Words

Across

1.
2.
3.
4.
5.
6.
7.
8.
9.
10.

Down

11.
12.
13.
14.
15.
16.
17.
18.

Diagonally

19.
20.

Other Word Forms

Across

21.
22.
23.
24.
25.

Down

26.
27.

Word search grid:

c o n s i d e r a b l y c o n t r a c t
a o u z w p r x n l p r o f i t p t o l
u s l g x n e v m d r e n d o w r d l d
t c t u h s e p o v e r t y c o o s u e
i i n e m t x t u z l w r b c d s e m s
o m q u a n t i t i e s a t u r p n n p
u h p r l p i x f m o c c u p i e s s q
s a u c e r a s v n x b t e y w r t q n
l u e o p o l i t i c s o h m n o i u l
y n d n c m o h l l e w r q v p u m a w
h t s f r i p r o f i t i n g u s a n y
a i h e x n w y q u a l i f y t a l t s
u l p r s e p v n b r b n i o q w i i t
n e q e n n e p r o b a b l e i d e t s
t r x n x t z n m c m c q u a l i t y c
e d s c h o l a r s h i p z n b s t x d
d m x e m o n u m e n t p r o s p e r p

G. Using Other Word Forms Write the Other Word Form that completes each series.

1. qualifies, _____ , qualifying
2. occupies, _____ , occupying
3. contracts, contracted, _____
4. confers, conferred, _____
5. prospers, _____ , prospering

H. Challenge Words Write the Challenge Word that completes each phrase.

crocodile	monotonous	molecule	pentagon	responsive

1. not varied, but _____
2. not a rectangle, but a _____
3. not an atom, but a _____
4. not an alligator, but a _____
5. not insensitive, but _____

I. Spelling and Writing Write *two* or more answers to each question. Use as many Spelling Words, Other Word Forms, and Challenge Words as you can. A few words are suggested. Proofread your work.

1. If you had to make up a story that no one would ever believe, what would you tell about?

   haunt – saucer – crocodile – pentagon – monument – molecule

2. How would you help a worthy candidate gain the office of class president?

   conference – politics – scholarship – qualify – responsive – considerably

3. What would you say if an interviewer asked you what kind of building or buildings your city or town needs?

   ought – occupy – contractor – quality – poverty – quantity

classify	effect	intellect	parallel	remedy
contractor	federal	liberate	politics	salary
delicate	indicate	monument	profess	sentiment
desperate	indifferent	occupy	qualify	venture
detour	initial	original	quantity	vessel

A. Columns and Rows Write Other Word Forms by adding letters to the spelling words. Use the graph to find the letters needed. If you need help, use the **Spelling Dictionary**.

	A	B	C	D	E
1		u	d	o	
2	a	e		i	n
3	v	l	s		y

1. vessel __
C3

2. remed __ __ __
D2 B2 C3

3. effect __ __ __
D2 A3 B2

4. profess __ __ __
D2 D1 E2

5. initial __ __
B3 E3

6. salar __ __ __
D2 B2 C3

7. sentiment __ __
A2 B3

8. indifferent __ __
B3 E3

9. indicat __ __ __
D2 D1 E2

10. venture __
C3

11. parallel __ __
B2 C1

12. federal __ __
B3 E3

13. politic __ __
A2 B3

14. occup __ __ __
D2 B2 C1

15. qualif __ __ __
D2 B2 C3

16. liberat __ __ __
D2 D1 E2

17. contractor __
C3

18. detour __ __
B2 C1

19. desperate __ __
B3 E3

20. intellect __ __ __
B1 A2 B3

21. classif __ __ __
D2 B2 C1

22. delicate __ __
B3 E3

23. original __ __
B3 E3

24. monument __ __
A2 B3

25. quantit __ __ __
D2 B2 C3

■ animated	★ considerably	▲ interval	◆ probable	○ session
appetite	escapade	irrigate	quality	situated
artificial	essay	levy	reference	specify
celebrate	excess	negligence	representative	specimen
columnist	international	principle	senate	succession

B. Two Extra Remove the two extra letters in each nonsense word. Write the remaining letters in order to complete the phrases with Other Word Forms of the spelling words. If you need help, use the **Spelling Dictionary**.

1. speacixfic   gave ○ _____ instructions

2. nsesvsions   two more court ○ _____

3. tnepglects   seldom ▲ _____ homework

4. mapupetites   healthy ■ _____

5. alevcied   ▲ _____ a fine

6. esodsays   writing English ★ _____

7. jsenkators   governors and ◆ _____

8. inctergvals   long ▲ _____ of time

9. jsituamtion   a funny ○ _____

10. sauccessior   a ○ _____ to the throne

11. kcolnumns   made ■ _____ and rows

12. pqualbities   having leadership ◆ _____

13. banimlation   the ■ _____ for a movie

14. celeybravtions   birthday ■ _____

15. mirriygated   ▲ _____ the land

16. bprinvciples   having strong ▲ _____

17. zprobhability   a slight ◆ _____

18. spekcipmens   laboratory ○ _____

19. grefervences   a list of ◆ _____

20. eswcaypades   several daring ★ _____

21. reparesenits   that ◆ _____ the people

22. linternationeally   is ★ _____ known

23. partidficially   not ■ _____ sweetened

24. conksiderpable   of ★ _____ difference

25. mexcessrive   an ★ _____ amount

■ graduate	★ ancestor	▲ conference	◆ interview	⬤ accurate
decade	adapted	blanketed	castaway	manager
scholarship	invest	wrestle	vegetate	gallery
candidate	mansion	temperate	ambulance	banister
destiny	annual	saucer	haunt	estimate

C. Newspaper Ads Complete each ad by writing Other Word Forms or the spelling words. If you need help, use the **Spelling Dictionary**.

1. Family reunion ad: Come and bring two ★ _____ along.

2. Senior class ad: We need someone famous to speak at ■ _____ .

3. Bakery ad: We ★ _____ our kneads to meet your needs.

4. Weather station ad: We need an announcer who predicts ⬤ _____ .

5. Play producer's ad: Don't miss the performance of the ■ _____ .

6. Circus ad: Several ◆ _____ are required for position of human cannonball.

7. Clockmaker's ad: A series of ▲ _____ are scheduled to see how time flies.

8. SOS ad: Bottles are desperately needed for some shipwrecked ◆ _____ .

9. Job opportunity ad: Two night ⬤ _____ are sought for ant farm.

10. Insurance company ad: A supply of ▲ _____ is needed to cover all losses.

11. Stock market ad: Our livestock guarantees a good ★ _____ .

12. Movie producer's ad: Volunteers for jungle movie are needed to ▲ _____ alligators.

13. Flying school ad: Several ■ _____ are available for free-falling classes.

14. Museum ad: Visit our two new ⬤ _____ of modern art.

15. Real estate ad: Buy two ★ _____ ; get a third one free.

16. Air conditioning ad: If you feel your ▲ _____ rising, you need us.

17. Gardener's ad: Growing your own ◆ _____ will sprout green thumbs.

18. Student government ad: We need ■ _____ for class president.

19. Leap-year committee ad: We meet ★ _____ , every fourth year.

20. Carpenter's ad: We build splinter-free ⬤ _____ .

21. Chauffeurs' ad: Leave the driving to us and reach your ■ _____ safely.

22. Hospital ad: Careful drivers are needed for six ◆ _____ .

23. Self-service restaurant ad: Bring your own cups and ▲ _____ .

24. Body shop ad: All ⬤ _____ are free with a fifty-dollar deposit.

25. Halloween store ad: We'll ◆ _____ you with our selection.

R
E
V
I
E
W

■ incident	★ ought	▲ attitude	◆ depot	● invisible
legislate	levee	individual	profiting	innocent
pressure	precious	official	execute	miserable
analyze	essence	cautiously	especially	prosperous
poverty	evidence	prominent	entrance	influence

D. Words in a Series Write Other Word Forms or the spelling words to complete each series. If you need help, use the **Spelling Dictionary**.

1. forces, pushes, ■ _____

2. clear, obvious, ★ _____

3. hidden, unseen, ● _____

4. neediness, poorness, ■ _____

5. independently, solely, ▲ _____

6. particularly, uniquely, ◆ _____

7. wealth, riches, ● _____

8. rivers, banks, ★ _____

9. events, occurrences, ■ _____

10. stations, terminals, ◆ _____

11. guiltless, blameless, ● _____

12. opinions, feelings, ▲ _____

13. senator, lawmaker, ■ _____

14. sadly, unfortunately, ● _____

15. persuades, dominates, ● _____

16. should, is obliged, ★ _____

17. rewarding, moneymaking, ◆ _____

18. lawfully, legally, ▲ _____

19. investigating, examining, ■ _____

20. valuable, cherished, ★ _____

21. doorways, lobbies, ◆ _____

22. mainly, noticeably, ▲ _____

23. accomplished, carried out, ◆ _____

24. core, idea, ★ _____

25. careful, watchful, ▲ _____

25

A. Pretest and Proofreading

B. Spelling Words and Phrases

1. **bullies**   afraid of <u>bullies</u>
2. **bullpen**   left the <u>bullpen</u>
3. **boulevard**   tree-lined <u>boulevard</u>
4. **instrument**   to play an <u>instrument</u>
5. **construction**   a <u>construction</u> worker
6. **interrupt**   shouldn't <u>interrupt</u> me
7. **industrial**   <u>industrial</u> training
8. **agricultural**   <u>agricultural</u> school
9. **uncomfortable**   <u>uncomfortable</u> feeling
10. **tongue**   bit my <u>tongue</u>
11. **smother**   to <u>smother</u> with care
12. **loveliness**   <u>loveliness</u> and charm
13. **governor**   <u>governor</u> of our state
14. **somersault**   a twisting <u>somersault</u>
15. **accompany**   will <u>accompany</u> you
16. **tough**   a <u>tough</u> decision
17. **roam**   to <u>roam</u> for days
18. **approach**   a new <u>approach</u>
19. **diploma**   received a <u>diploma</u>
20. **though**   <u>though</u> we tried

Other Word Forms

> bully, bullied
> bullpens
> boulevards
> instrumental
> construct, constructed
> interrupting, interruption
> industry, industries
> agriculture, agriculturally
> comfort, uncomfortably
> tongues
> smothered
> love, lovely
> govern, government
> somersaults
> accompanies, accompanying
> tougher, toughen
> roamed
> approaching
> diplomas

C. Challenge Words and Phrases

1. **multiples**   <u>multiples</u> of six
2. **subtle**   a <u>subtle</u> difference
3. **mustache**   trimmed the <u>mustache</u>
4. **punctuation**   forgot the <u>punctuation</u>
5. **publishers**   several book <u>publishers</u>

D. Crossword Puzzle Solve the puzzle by writing all the words from the spelling list. Check your answers in the **Spelling Dictionary**.

Across
1. a gymnastic exercise
4. a wide street
7. however
8. a method
10. the head of a state
12. uneasy
13. strong
14. having to do with farming
17. relating to industry
18. beauty
19. to break in on

Down
2. to suffocate
3. a part of the mouth
4. where baseball pitchers warm up
5. a degree earned from a school
6. the process of building something
9. to wander
11. people who pick on weaker people
15. a device for producing music
16. to go with

Spelling Words

bullies bullpen boulevard instrument construction
interrupt industrial agricultural uncomfortable
tongue smother loveliness governor somersault
accompany tough roam approach diploma though

E. Sort Your Words In alphabetical order, write the spelling words under the correct headings. If you need help, use the **Spelling Dictionary**.

**Words with
One Syllable**

1. _____   3. _____
2. _____   4. _____

**Words with
Two Syllables**

5. _____   7. _____
6. _____   8. _____

**Words with
Three Syllables**

9. _____   13. _____
10. _____   14. _____
11. _____   15. _____
12. _____   16. _____

**Words with
Four Syllables**

17. _____   18. _____

**Words with
Five Syllables**

19. _____   20. _____

F. Spinner Words Spin the letters in each scrambled word to uncover a word in the spelling list. Write the correct word.

1. gueton
2. ghtou
3. saultsomer
4. fortableuncom
5. plomadi
6. proachap
7. amro
8. trialindus
9. thersmo
10. liesbul

11. ruptinter
12. penbull
13. ernorgov
14. panyaccom
15. oughth
16. linesslove
17. culturalagri
18. uctionconstr
19. vardboule
20. umentinstr

G. Using Other Word Forms Write the Other Word Form that completes each sentence.

1. This company has tight security. A guard always _____ (accompany) each visitor.
2. The little girl was happy to find her lost doll. She _____ (smother) it with kisses.
3. They built a new shed. They _____ (construction) a small building.
4. The big dog tormented the puppy. He _____ (bullies) him.
5. She kept cutting him off. She had a habit of _____ (interrupt) conversations.

H. Challenge Words Write the Challenge Word that completes each sentence.

multiples	subtle	mustache	punctuation	publishers

1. If the companies produce books, they may be _____ .
2. If something is difficult to detect, it may be very _____ .
3. If the numbers end with zero, they are _____ of ten.
4. If the sentence has no commas or period, it may require _____ .
5. If it is hair that grows above the upper lip, it probably is a _____ .

I. Spelling and Writing Write *two* or more answers to each question. Use as many Spelling Words, Other Word Forms, and Challenge Words as you can. A few words are suggested. Proofread your work.

1. How would you feel if some students from your school were causing trouble at a school baseball game?

   bullies – bullpen – interrupt – tough – subtle

2. What would you ask if you found out that the state is planning to build a new highway near your home?

   boulevard – construction – industrial – governor – agricultural – loveliness

3. What would you like to know before you signed up for a gymnastics class?

   accompany – multiples – approach – uncomfortable – somersault – diploma

26

A. Pretest and Proofreading

B. Spelling Words and Phrases

1. **tariff**   paid the <u>tariff</u>
2. **harried**   a <u>harried</u> expression
3. **character**   a <u>character</u> in the play
4. **embarrassment**   red with <u>embarrassment</u>
5. **comparatively**   <u>comparatively</u> weak
6. **popularity**   not a <u>popularity</u> contest
7. **parcel**   wrapped the <u>parcel</u>
8. **startle**   would <u>startle</u> me
9. **jarring**   <u>jarring</u> sound
10. **darkened**   <u>darkened</u> room
11. **carnival**   rides at the <u>carnival</u>
12. **marvelous**   a <u>marvelous</u> time
13. **marginal**   only a <u>marginal</u> job
14. **guardian**   appointed a <u>guardian</u>
15. **departure**   <u>departure</u> time
16. **enlargement**   <u>enlargement</u> of the photo
17. **sanitary**   <u>sanitary</u> conditions
18. **satellite**   <u>satellite</u> in orbit
19. **gradually**   <u>gradually</u> came to a stop
20. **practically**   <u>practically</u> finished

C. Challenge Words and Phrases

1. **parliament**   elected to <u>parliament</u>
2. **disregarding**   <u>disregarding</u> the facts
3. **regardless**   <u>regardless</u> of the time
4. **parachute**   the open <u>parachute</u>
5. **sarcastic**   a <u>sarcastic</u> remark

Other Word Forms

> tariffs
> harry, harries
> characteristic
> embarrass
> compare, comparative
> popular
> parcels, parceled
> startling
> jar, jarred
> dark, darken
> carnivals
> marvel, marveled,
>   marvelously
> margin, marginally
> guard, guardedly
> depart
> large, enlarge, enlarging
> sanitize, sanitation
> satellites
> grade, gradual
> practice, practical

D. Break the Code Use the code to write the spelling words.

a	b	c	d	e	f	g	h	i	j	k	l	m	n	o	p	q	r	s	t	u	v	w	x	y	z
↓	↓	↓	↓	↓	↓	↓	↓	↓	↓	↓	↓	↓	↓	↓	↓	↓	↓	↓	↓	↓	↓	↓	↓	↓	↓
x	h	l	q	t	a	e	w	m	b	r	o	d	i	f	s	u	c	z	g	n	y	j	p	k	v

1. wfkknut
2. bfkkngm
3. rbfkfregk
4. xkfrenrfccv
5. mgxfkeqkg
6. gucfktgigue
7. rfkunzfc
8. tqfkmnfu
9. gijfkkfppigue
10. mfkygugm

11. xfkrgc
12. efknoo
13. pfegccneg
14. pefkecg
15. xlxqcfknev
16. ifkzgclqp
17. tkfmqfccv
18. pfunefkv
19. ifktnufc
20. rlixfkfenzgcv

E. Complete the Equations Write each of the spelling words to complete the equations.

1. dirty ≠
2. likability =
3. calm ≠
4. package =
5. dimmed =
6. pride ≠
7. moon =
8. alarm =
9. shrinkage ≠
10. barely acceptable =

11. arrival ≠
12. festival =
13. almost =
14. reputation =
15. steadying ≠
16. terrible ≠
17. suddenly ≠
18. relatively =
19. tax =
20. protector =

Spelling Words

tariff harried character embarrassment comparatively
popularity parcel startle jarring darkened
carnival marvelous marginal guardian departure
enlargement satellite sanitary gradually practically

F. Base Words The spelling list contains seven base words and thirteen words that are not base words. Write each spelling word.

Words That Are Not Base Words	Base Words
1. parcels	_____
2. characteristic	_____
3. startling	_____
4. carnivals	_____
5. tariffs	_____
6. sanitize	_____
7. satellites	_____
8. _____	jar
9. _____	harry
10. _____	margin
11. _____	grade
12. _____	embarrass
13. _____	guard
14. _____	popular
15. _____	practice
16. _____	compare
17. _____	large
18. _____	depart
19. _____	dark
20. _____	marvel

G. Using Other Word Forms Write the Other Word Form that completes each sentence.

1. To do something wonderfully is to do it _____ (marvelous).
2. To just barely win the race is to win _____ (marginal).
3. A feature or quality of something is a _____ (character).
4. To keep the area clean is to practice _____ (sanitary).
5. The moons that orbit planets are _____ (satellite).

H. Challenge Words Write the Challenge Word that completes each analogy.

parliament	disregarding	regardless	parachute	sarcastic

1. **however** is to **nevertheless** as **despite everything** is to _____
2. **playful** is to **whimsical** as **scornful** is to _____
3. **ship** is to **life preserver** as **airplane** is to _____
4. **United States** is to **congress** as **Canada** is to _____
5. **loving** is to **cherishing** as **ignoring** is to _____

I. Spelling and Writing Write each set of words in a sentence. You may use Other Word Forms. Proofread your work.

1. marginal – sanitary – comparatively
2. popularity – character – practically
3. startle – jarring – embarrassment
4. harried – parcel – tariff
5. guardian – marvelous – carnival
6. satellite – enlargement – darkened
7. departure – gradually – dark
8. parliament – sarcastic – disregarding
9. regardless – parachute – startling

27

A. Pretest and Proofreading

B. Spelling Words and Phrases

1. **experiment** — a science <u>experiment</u>
2. **prosperity** — health and <u>prosperity</u>
3. **ceremony** — wedding <u>ceremony</u>
4. **certificate** — an owner's <u>certificate</u>
5. **germs** — <u>germs</u> that cause disease
6. **nervous** — a <u>nervous</u> giggle
7. **service** — <u>service</u> in the cafeteria
8. **vertically** — horizontally or <u>vertically</u>
9. **prefer** — would <u>prefer</u> to eat here
10. **reserve** — to <u>reserve</u> a seat
11. **determine** — to <u>determine</u> the value
12. **commercial** — TV <u>commercial</u>
13. **anniversary** — twelfth <u>anniversary</u>
14. **university** — <u>university</u> students
15. **percentage** — a high <u>percentage</u>
16. **either** — <u>either</u> way
17. **generous** — a <u>generous</u> offer
18. **circumference** — <u>circumference</u> of a circle
19. **birth** — place of <u>birth</u>
20. **confirm** — to <u>confirm</u> the reservation

C. Challenge Words and Phrases

1. **submerged** — <u>submerged</u> or surfaced
2. **mercury** — <u>mercury</u> thermometer
3. **mediocre** — a <u>mediocre</u> effort
4. **emergency** — take <u>emergency</u> action
   furthermore — find and, <u>furthermore</u>, study

Other Word Forms

experimental
prosper, prosperous
ceremonies, ceremonial
certify, certified,
   certification
germ, germy
nerve, nervousness
services, serviced
vertical
preferred, preference
reserving, reservation
determined, determination
commerce, commercially,
   commercialism
anniversaries
universe, universities
percent
generosity
circumferences
births
confirmed, confirmation

D. Cause and Effect Write the words from the spelling list to complete the sentences.

1. If you celebrate once a year, you could be having an _____ .
2. If a company wishes to advertise on TV, it makes a _____ .
3. If you want to see whether you have the correct flight with an airline, you should _____ your reservation.
4. If you know the radius of a circle, you can compute the _____ .
5. If it is the first day of your life, it is the day of your _____ .
6. If people share with you, they are being _____ .
7. If you are a caterer, you often provide food and _____ after a wedding _____ .
8. If you want to prove a scientific law, you do an _____ .
9. If you complete a course, you may receive a _____ for it.
10. If you have an even choice of two items, you could choose _____ one.
11. If you tell the librarians to save a book for you, they will _____ it.
12. If times are good in the country, there is a feeling of _____ .
13. If a line is drawn up and down, it is drawn _____ .
14. If you use disinfectant, you are concerned about _____ .
15. If you want to leave a tip in a restaurant, you should figure out a _____ of your bill.
16. If you are not feeling calm, you are probably feeling _____ .
17. If you want to go to a large school which includes many colleges, you will choose a _____ .
18. If you like a gray sweat shirt rather than a white one, you _____ the gray.
19. If you want to solve a problem, you must first _____ the cause of it.

Spelling Words

*experiment prosperity ceremony certificate germs
nervous service vertically prefer reserve determine
commercial anniversary university percentage
either generous circumference birth confirm*

E. Word Parts

Add a Suffix Add a suffix to each word to write a word from the spelling list. For some words, you will need to add or subtract a letter, or both, before adding the suffix.

1. universe
2. nerve
3. percent
4. germ

5. vertical
6. commerce
7. prosper

Subtract a Suffix Subtract a suffix from each word to write a word from the spelling list. For some words, you will need to add, subtract, or change letters to find the base word.

8. confirmation
9. ceremonies
10. reservation
11. determination
12. experimental
13. servicing

14. preference
15. certification
16. generosity
17. births
18. anniversaries

19. Write the two words that were not used.

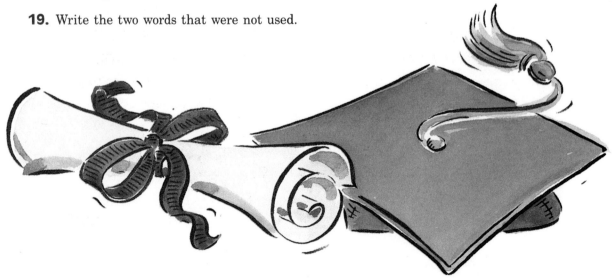

F. Using Other Word Forms Write the Other Word Form that fits each clue.

1. very successful _____ (prosperity)
2. yearly events _____ (anniversary)
3. something that proves the truth _____ (confirm)
4. arrangement made to secure a place _____ (reserve)
5. liking something more than something else _____ (prefer)

G. Challenge Words Write the Challenge Word that replaces each underlined word or phrase.

submerged	mercury	mediocre	emergency	furthermore

1. The hotel food was <u>ordinary</u>.
2. We agree with you; <u>moreover</u>, we will support you.
3. The submarine was <u>below the surface</u>.
4. We use <u>a metallic element</u> inside our thermometers.
5. The hurricane created the <u>serious situation</u>.

H. Spelling and Writing Use each phrase in a sentence. You may want to use the words in a different order or use Other Word Forms. Proofread for spelling using one of the Proofreading Tips from the Yellow Pages.

1. conducted an <u>experiment</u>
2. a time of <u>prosperity</u>
3. attended the <u>ceremony</u>
4. a teaching <u>certificate</u>
5. protect us from <u>germs</u>
6. <u>nervous</u> about the test
7. a cleaning <u>service</u>
8. arranged <u>vertically</u>
9. the food we <u>prefer</u>
10. <u>reserve</u> a table
11. will <u>determine</u> our pay
12. a <u>commercial</u> success
13. wedding <u>anniversary</u>
14. attended a <u>university</u>
15. a <u>percentage</u> of the total
16. <u>either</u> one or two
17. a <u>generous</u> person
18. <u>circumference</u> and area
19. the <u>birth</u> of the child
20. <u>confirm</u> the meeting

28

A. Pretest and Proofreading

B. Spelling Words and Phrases

1. **orbit** — Earth's orbit
2. ~~**ordinary**~~ — ordinary meal
3. **organism** — harmless organism
4. **organization** — needs some organization
5. **formal** — formal statement
6. **formerly** — formerly unknown
7. **forfeit** — will forfeit my turn
8. **fortunate** — fortunate choice
9. **horror** — horror movie
10. **horrifying** — horrifying story
11. **horrid** — horrid joke
12. **torrid** — a torrid region
13. **torment** — torment of a sunburn
14. **portion** — smaller portion
15. **cornerstone** — cornerstone of a building
16. **correspond** — to correspond by mail
17. **gorgeous** — gorgeous scenery
18. **glorious** — glorious sunrise
19. **chorus** — the school chorus
20. **sorrowful** — a sorrowful sigh

Other Word Forms

orbited
ordinarily
organ, organisms, organic
organize
formality
former
forfeited
fortune, fortunately
horrors, horrible
horrify, horrifies
horridly
torridly
tormented, tormenting
portions, portioned
cornerstones
corresponded,
   correspondence
gorgeously
glory, gloried, gloriously
choruses
sorrow, sorrowfully

C. Challenge Words and Phrases

1. **formidable** — a formidable foe
2. **tortoise** — the plodding tortoise
3. **forefathers** — forefathers of the family
4. **tornadoes** — violence of tornadoes
5. **porcupine** — the prickly porcupine

D. Of O's and R's In alphabetical order, write the spelling words under the correct headings. One word goes in more than one place.

Double *r* Following an *o*		Single *r* Following an *o*		
1. ____	4. ____	7. ____	12. ____	17. ____
2. ____	5. ____	8. ____	13. ____	18. ____
3. ____	6. ____	9. ____	14. ____	19. ____
		10. ____	15. ____	20. ____
		11. ____	16. ____	21. ____

E. Antonyms Write the word from the spelling list that is an antonym for each word.

1. uncommon
2. gain
3. homely
4. unlucky
5. casual
6. happy
7. pleasant
8. cold
9. shameful

F. Synonyms Write the word from the spelling list that is a synonym for each word.

1. path
2. pain
3. choir
4. communicate
5. being
6. terrifying
7. group
8. foundation
9. terror
10. beforehand
11. part

Spelling Words

orbit ordinary organism organization formal
formerly forfeit fortunate horror horrifying
horrid torrid torment portion cornerstone
correspond gorgeous glorious chorus sorrowful

G. Guide Words These word pairs could appear as guide words in a dictionary. Write the words from the spelling list that would appear on the same page as each pair of guide words.

bullpen–circumference
1. ____

continuous–define
2. ____   3. ____

fail–generally
4. ____   6. ____
5. ____   7. ____

generate–harried
8. ____   9. ____

harry–incident
10. ____   12. ____
11. ____

negligence–organize
13. ____   15. ____
14. ____   16. ____

plentiful–proceed
17. ____

slumber–summon
18. ____

suppose–uncommon
19. ____   20. ____

'sing Other Word Forms Add an ending to each adjective to make it an adverb.
'te this Other Word Form to complete each phrase.

1. h‍ective   **Adverb**

2. glori‍   behaved _____

3. gorgeou‍   sang _____ in the chorus

4. sorrowful   was dressed _____

5. ordinary   cried _____

_____ on time

I. **Challenge Words** ‍

_____the Challenge Word that fits each group of words.

formidable	torto‍	forefathers	tornadoes	porcupine

1. scales, shell, land turtle, _____

2. relatives, deceased, ancestors, ‍

3. rodent, spines, quills, _____

4. stormy, winds, twisting, _____

5. awesome, strong, difficult, _____

J. **Spelling and Writing** Write each set of words
Other Word Forms. Proofread for spelling using o‍sentence. You may use
from the Yellow Pages.   ‍he Proofreading Tips

1. horrifying, cornerstone, ordinary

2. portion, forfeit, gorgeous

3. orbit, portion, glorious

4. horror, torment, organism

5. fortunate, organization, formal

6. horrid, formerly, chorus

7. sorrowful, correspondence, formal

8. organization, correspond, ordinary

9. formerly, horrified, torrid

29

A. Pretest and Proofreading

B. Spelling Words and Phrases

1. editor — editor of the magazine
2. excellent — excellent recommendation
3. exception — only one exception
4. excessive — excessive speed
5. executive — executive offices
6. effective — an effective speaker
7. benefits — if it benefits everyon
8. decimal — a decimal fractic
9. senator — wrote to the se
10. register — to register
11. recognize — failed t restaurant
12. restaurant — a cr ul crop
13. plentiful — igh temperature
14. temperature — has no regret
15. regret — professor of biology
16. professor — to misspell one word
17. misspell — fond memories
18. mem able — memorable occasion
19. morial — a memorial service
20

Other Wor al
edit, celled
exc
ess, excesses
ecute, executives
effect, effectively
benefit, beneficial
decimals
senate
registration
recognizing, recognition
restaurants
plenty
temper, temperate
regretted, regretful
profess, professes
spell, misspelled
memory, memorize,
  memorizing
memorably
memorialize

allenge Words and Phrases

1. detector — the metal detector
2. architecture — modern architecture
3. confederacy — members of the confederacy
4. objective — the main objective
5. cellophane — wrapped in cellophane

D. Ending Sounds Write the words from the spelling list that have the same ending sounds as the words below.

1. forget
2. pictorial ____
3. bountiful ____
4. warrant ____
5. detective ____

____

6. dyes ____
7. creditor ____

____

____

Spelling Words

8. favorable ____
9. deception ____
10. repel ____
11. categories ____
12. semester ____
13. legislature ____
14. repellent ____
15. forfeits ____
16. normal ____

E. Missing Vowels Find the missing vowels and write the spelling words.

1. m __ ssp __ ll
2. r __ gr __ t
3. r __ c __ gn __ z __
4. __ xc __ ll __ nt
5. d __ c __ m __ l
6. pl __ nt __ f __ l
7. __ xc __ pt __ __ n
8. s __ n __ t __ r
9. __ x __ c __ t __ v __
10. r __ st __ __ r __ nt
11. m __ m __ r __ __ l
12. b __ n __ f __ ts
13. __ xc __ ss __ v __
14. __ d __ t __ r
15. r __ g __ st __ r
16. __ ff __ ct __ v __
17. t __ mp __ r __ t __ r __
18. m __ m __ r __ __ s
19. pr __ f __ ss __ r
20. m __ m __ r __ bl __

Spelling Words

editor   excellent   exception   excessive   executiv
effective   benefits   decimal   senator   registe
recognize   restaurant   plentiful   temperatu   regret
professor   misspell   memories   memorable   memorial

F. Be a Sentence Detective Unscramble the words under each blank. Write each unscrambled word.

1. The state _____ disagreed with the _____ branch of the government on a
tax issue. nesator   cuexeivte

2. The newspaper _____ became a journalism _____ at the college.
deitor   fopressor

3. I _____ the name on the _____ plaque.
ercongize   emmroail

4. The host requested everyone to sign the guest _____ on this
gistrere
_____ occasion.
amemblero

5. With the _____ of turnips most of the crops were _____ .
cptexeoin   plneitful

6. My brother may _____ that he does not understand _____ fractions.
ergrte   medical

7. The student had written an _____ paper describing her childhood _____ .
xecentlle   mimeores

8. We were irritable because of the _____ humidity and high _____ .
xecssevie   mpetreature

9. Regular exercise is _____ in providing _____ to your health.
ffectieve   nebeitsf

10. Did the _____ owner _____ a word on this menu?
estraurnta   ellspmis

G. Using Other Word Forms Write the Other Word Form that completes each sentence.

1. If it is helpful, it is _____ (benefits).

2. If you were sorry for something, you _____ (regret) it.

3. If I produced the desired result, I have done it _____ (effective).

4. If you are acknowledged for something, you have received _____ (recognize).

5. If you are learning it by heart, you are _____ (memories) it.

H. Challenge Words Write the Challenge Word that completes each phrase.

detector	architecture	confederacy	objective	cellophane

1. either the goal or the _____

2. either an alliance or a _____

3. either a seismograph or a _____

4. either plastic wrap or _____

5. either a building design or _____

I. Spelling and Writing Write two or more questions about each statement. Use as many Spelling Words, Other Word Forms, and Challenge Words as you can. A few words are suggested. Proofread for spelling using one of the Proofreading Tips from the Yellow Pages.

1. A famous member of Congress has retired.
senator   executive   excellent   register   regret   memory
objectives   restaurant

Example: Do the <u>senators</u> believe she was an <u>excellent</u> business <u>executive</u>?

2. The school newspaper staff was under pressure to meet its deadline.
editor   misspell   temper   recognize   excessive
memorable   effective

3. A statue was unveiled in front of the college building.
professor   memorial   registration   architecture
confederacy   exceptional

30

■ agricultural   ★ commercial   ▲ forfeit   ◆ misspell   ○ smother
approach   correspond   formal   nervous   startle
boulevard   darkened   glorious   orbit   tariff
carnival   determine   industrial   organism   tongue
circumference   experiment   memories   recognize   torment

A. Chain Reaction

Write Other Word Forms by using the clues to complete the chain of words. Notice that the boxed letter of each answer is the *first* letter of the next answer. If you need help, use the **Spelling Dictionary**.

1. used to lick stamps ○ _ _ □ _ _ _ _
2. anxiously ◆ _ □ _ _ _ _ _ _ _
3. lab tests ★ _ _ _ _ _ _ _ □ _ _ _ _
4. a remembered event ▲ _ _ _ _ □ _ _
5. planets' paths ◆ _ _ □ _ _ _
6. wide city streets ■ _ _ _ _ _ _ _ □ _ _ _
7. farming ■ _ _ _ _ _ _ _ _ □ _ _ _
8. taxes on imports and exports ○ _ _ _ _ _ □ _ _
9. gave up ▲ _ _ _ _ _ _ □ _ _ _
10. manufacturing ▲ _ _ □ _ _ _ _ _ _
11. found out precisely ★ _ _ □ _ _ _ _ _ _ _
12. caused great pain ○ _ □ □ _ _ _ _ _ _ _ _
13. living things ◆ _ _ □ _ _ _ _ _ _
14. magnificently ▲ _ _ _ □ _ _ _ _ _ _
15. identified ◆ _ _ □ _ _ _ _ _ _
16. circuses ■ □ □ _ _ _ _ _ _ _
17. wrote letters ★ □ _ _ _ _ _ _ _ _ _ _ _ _
18. distances around circles ■ _ _ _ _ _ _ _ □ _ _ _ _ _ _
19. officially ▲ _ _ _ _ □ _ _ _
20. came nearer ■ _ _ _ _ _ _ _ □ _ _ _
21. TV ads ★ _ _ _ _ □ _ _ _ _ _ _
22. a word written incorrectly ◆ _ _ _ □ _ _ _ _ _ _ _
23. suffocates ○ □ _ _ _ _ _ _ _ _
24. shocked ○ _ _ _ _ _ _ _ _ □
25. to grow cloudy ★ _ _ _ _ _ _ _

R
E
V
I
E
W

■ accompany	★ diploma	▲ roam	◆ construction	◉ enlargement
jarring	popularity	departure	parcel	reserve
percentage	service	plentiful	confirm	interrupt
senator	anniversary	birth	marginal	embarrassment
portion	organization	professor	somersault	character

B. Not the Way It Was Planned

Write Other Word Forms or the spelling words to complete these phrases about unexpected or unfortunate happenings. If you need help, use the **Spelling Dictionary**.

1. plumbers ◆ _____ the bathroom on the front porch

2. realizing your ◉ _____ seats are behind the stage

3. parents ■ _____ you to your first school dance

4. finding your pet tarantula ▲ _____ around the kitchen

5. blank ★ _____ being handed out at graduation

6. being ■ _____ out of your seat by an earthquake

7. sending photos to be ◉ _____ and receiving them reduced

8. delivering two ◆ _____ to the wrong address

9. being voted most ★ _____ only because you have a pool

10. ▲ _____ for France in a canoe instead of an ocean liner

11. scoring one hundred ■ _____ and having to take the test over

12. traffic ◉ _____ a road race

13. being told that your hotel ◆ _____ the wrong reservation date

14. needing your television to be ★ _____ and not being able to afford the repair

15. being short of money when you thought you had ▲ _____

16. forgetting to introduce the two visiting ■ _____ to the class

17. being told to make ◆ _____ and not having a ruler

18. wearing two different shoes and feeling ◉ _____

19. finding the wrong date on your ▲ _____ certificate

20. arriving for your parents' ★ _____ party a week early

21. dropping the last two ■ _____ of pie before you had any

22. completing four perfect ◆ _____ and having no one see them

23. ★ _____ a picnic and forgetting about the food

24. interrupting a meeting of college ▲ _____

25. playing two ◉ _____ in a play and mixing up your lines

■ chorus   ★ excellent   ▲ gradually   ◆ memorial   ○ temperature

chorus	excellent	gradually	memorial	temperature
comparatively	exception	guardian	ordinary	torrid
decimal	formerly	harried	prefer	tough
editor	generous	horrifying	regret	uncomfortable
effective	germs	memorable	sorrowful	university

C. Slash Away Remove one letter from each word. Then join the remaining letters to write an Other Word Form for each spelling word. If you need help, use the **Spelling Dictionary**.

1. it rough best = ○ _____

2. harp rye = ▲ _____

3. deck rim ails = ■ _____

4. pore fear read = ◆ _____

5. word tin are it lay = ◆ _____

6. chop rushes = ■ _____

7. fort my her = ★ _____

8. fed sit ores = ■ _____

9. red great fuel lay = ◆ _____

10. hex ace pat lion ail = ★ _____

11. men moral be lye = ▲ _____

12. team pear ate up rest = ○ _____

13. me off we cat wed = ■ _____

14. he ax ace ill fence = ★ _____

15. fun come four tabs lay = ○ _____

16. come part his one = ■ _____

17. gram duals = ▲ _____

18. guards it ants = ▲ _____

19. age near out slay = ★ _____

20. unit verse wit pies = ○ _____

21. gear me = ★ _____

22. torn ride lye = ○ _____

23. met mop ray = ◆ _____

24. horn rim fired = ▲ _____

25. sort grows = ◆ _____

■ bullies	★ governor	▲ loveliness	◆ marvelous	● though
practically	prosperity	vertically	certificate	satellite
fortunate	horrid	cornerstone	horror	gorgeous
ceremony	excessive	instrument	sanitary	executive
benefits	restaurant	register	either	bullpen

D. Words in a Series

Write Other Word Forms or the spelling words to complete each series. If you need help, use the **Spelling Dictionary**.

1. teaser, tormentor, ■ _____

2. attractive, charming, ▲ _____

3. senators, mayors, ★ _____

4. however, even, ● _____

5. wonderfully, astonishingly, ◆ _____

6. usable, workable, ■ _____

7. succeeds, gains, ★ _____

8. documents, diplomas, ◆ _____

9. upright, straight, ▲ _____

10. moon, orbiting body, ● _____

11. luckily, happily, ■ _____

12. fears, terrors, ◆ _____

13. disagreeable, unpleasant, ★ _____

14. foundations, building blocks, ▲ _____

15. splendidly, dazzlingly, ● _____

16. rite, ritual, ■ _____

17. clean, disinfect, ◆ _____

18. tools, devices, ▲ _____

19. extremely, exceedingly, ★ _____

20. managers, administrators, ● _____

21. helped, favored, ■ _____

22. enrolled, recorded, ▲ _____

23. cafés, diners, ★ _____

24. baseball, dugout, ● _____

25. one, each, ◆ _____

31

A. Pretest and Proofreading

B. Spelling Words and Phrases

1. vicinity — in this vicinity
2. literacy — literacy test
3. pigeon — wings of the pigeon
4. religion — study of religion
5. opinion — each one's opinion
6. omission — omission of a word
7. commission — athletic commission
8. decision — difficult decision
9. position — to apply for the position
10. disposition — unpleasant disposition
11. composition — a brief composition
12. condition — in excellent condition
13. definition — a dictionary definition
14. ammunition — to supply with ammunition
15. description — written description
16. anticipate — to anticipate the results
17. refrigerate — to refrigerate until ready
18. captivity — held in captivity
19. particularly — particularly soft
20. possibilities — exciting possibilities

Other Word Forms

vicinities
literate, literature
pigeons
religions
opinionated
omit, omitted, omissions
commissions
commit, committing
decide, deciding, decisions
positions
dispose, disposing
compose, compositions
conditioned, conditionally
define, defining
ammunitions
describe, descriptive
anticipating, anticipation
refrigerator, refrigeration
captive
particular, particulars
possible, possibility

C. Challenge Words and Phrases

1. chimpanzee — the noisy chimpanzee
2. illiterate — will not remain illiterate
3. misspelled — frequently misspelled
4. discrimination — unlawful discrimination
5. instinctively — acted instinctively

D. Missing Vowels Find the missing vowels and write the spelling words.

1. r __ fr __ g __ r __ t __
2. p __ ss __ b __ l __ t __ __ s
3. d __ c __ s __ __ n
4. v __ c __ n __ t __
5. __ m __ ss __ __ n
6. l __ t __ r __ c __
7. c __ nd __ t __ __ n
8. __ p __ n __ __ n
9. d __ f __ n __ t __ __ n
10. __ mm __ n __ t __ __ n
11. p __ rt __ c __ l __ rl __
12. d __ sp __ s __ t __ __ n
13. r __ l __ g __ __ n
14. p __ s __ t __ __ n
15. __ nt __ c __ p __ t __
16. p __ g __ __ n
17. c __ mp __ s __ t __ __ n
18. c __ pt __ v __ t __
19. c __ mm __ ss __ __ n
20. d __ scr __ pt __ __ n

E. Sort Your Words In alphabetical order, write the spelling words under the correct headings.

Words Ending in *ion*		Words Ending in *ate*		Words Ending in *y*	
1. _____	7. _____	13. _____	14. _____	15. _____	17. _____
2. _____	8. _____			16. _____	18. _____
3. _____	9. _____				
4. _____	10. _____				
5. _____	11. _____				
6. _____	12. _____				

19. Write the two words that did not fit anywhere.

Spelling Words

vicinity literacy pigeon religion opinion
omission commission decision position disposition
composition condition definition ammunition
description anticipate refrigerate captivity
particularly possibilities

F. Sentence Detective Unscramble the word under each blank. Write each unscrambled word in the sentence.

1. The lawyers _____ a _____ from the jury soon.
                 citetapina   donesici

2. He claims that a _____ can have a gloomy _____ .
                nogeip   isdspotoini

3. The article was a well-researched _____ of animals in _____ .
                     sedcrpitoin   iacptivty

4. Your _____ is about a _____ amusing topic.
     ocmpotsioni   lypratciular

5. Taking a _____ test is a _____ of acceptance to the private school.
       ilcrtaey   indociont

6. Is it your _____ to _____ the bread before baking it?
        ipoinon   eerftregriat

7. By _____ , a cartridge is a type of _____ .
    ifedintion   nmmauitoin

8. The suggestions offered by this year's student _____ provided several
                                       icommsoins
_____ for fund-raising.
 isspoibliteis

9. People once living in this _____ practiced a mysterious _____ .
                   ivinicty   lerigion

10. The _____ of facts in your debate made your _____ weak.
     missoino   ioopsitn

G. Using Other Word Forms
Write the Other Word Form that completes each sentence.

1. His _____ (anticipate) of tomorrow's test was keeping him awake.
2. The student wrote a _____ (description) paragraph about the characteristics of rock formations.
3. She only _____ (condition) gave her approval. She wanted certain demands met before she fully agreed.
4. He strongly expressed his views on every issue. He is an _____ (opinion) person.
5. His name was not on the list. It was _____ (omission) by mistake.

H. Challenge Words
Write the Challenge Word that completes each sentence.

chimpanzee	illiterate	misspelled	discrimination	instinctively

1. People who respond without thinking may be reacting _____ .
2. Someone who cannot read is said to be _____ .
3. Students who scored poorly in spelling _____ many words.
4. A person who is prejudiced could be guilty of _____ .
5. A veterinarian for a zoo might be asked to treat a _____ .

I. Spelling and Writing
Write each set of words in a sentence. You may use Other Word Forms. Proofread for spelling using one of the Proofreading Tips from the Yellow Pages.

1. omission, condition, particularly
2. definition, religion, anticipate
3. position, vicinity, refrigerator
4. literacy, commission, decision
5. possibilities, captivity, pigeon
6. ammunition, disposition, opinion
7. description, composition, position
8. anticipate, possibilities, condition
9. decision, description, opinion

32

A. Pretest and Proofreading

B. Spelling Words and Phrases

1. **improvise** — to <u>improvise</u> on stage
2. **civilized** — <u>civilized</u> behavior
3. **distinct** — <u>distinct</u> outline
4. **similar** — <u>similar</u> thoughts
5. **singular** — <u>singular</u> or plural
6. **sincerely** — <u>sincerely</u> sorry
7. **signature** — wrote my <u>signature</u>
8. **literature** — modern <u>literature</u>
9. **committee** — <u>committee</u> member
10. **ambition** — an <u>ambition</u> to succeed
11. **assistance** — need your <u>assistance</u>
12. **resistance** — <u>resistance</u> to rust
13. **existence** — daily <u>existence</u>
14. **equipped** — <u>equipped</u> the gym
15. **equipment** — camera <u>equipment</u>
16. **sufficient** — a <u>sufficient</u> supply
17. **magnificent** — a <u>magnificent</u> view
18. **distinguished** — a <u>distinguished</u> author
19. **delicious** — three <u>delicious</u> pears
20. **continuous** — a <u>continuous</u> line

Other Word Forms

improvising, improvisation
civil, civilizing
distinctly, distinctive
similarly, similarity
single, singularly
sincere
sign, signer
literate, literary
commit, committed,
  committees
ambitions, ambitious
assist, assistant
resist
exist, existing
equip, equips, equipping
suffice, sufficiently
magnificently,
  magnificence
distinguish, distinguishing
deliciously
continue, continuation

C. Challenge Words and Phrases

1. **edible** — <u>edible</u> roots
2. **conspicuous** — a <u>conspicuous</u> mistake
3. **irresistible** — <u>irresistible</u> offer
4. **dimensions** — <u>dimensions</u> of the room
5. **penicillin** — treated with <u>penicillin</u>

D. Base Words The spelling list contains five base words and fifteen words that are not base words. Write each spelling word.

Words That Are Not Base Words	Base Words		Words That Are Not Base Words	Base Words
1. deliciously	_____		**11.** _____	assist
2. distinctive	_____		**12.** _____	sincere
3. similarity	_____		**13.** _____	literate
4. improvisation	_____		**14.** _____	sign
5. ambitious	_____		**15.** _____	single
6. _____	magnify		**16.** _____	civil
7. _____	continue		**17.** _____	equip
8. _____	suffice			
9. _____	exist		**18.** _____	commit
10. _____	resist		**19.** _____	distinguish

E. Generally Speaking Write each spelling word in the group it best fits.

1. aid, help, _____

2. same, alike, _____

3. tools, supplies, _____

4. group, members, _____

5. create, make do, _____

6. honestly, earnestly, _____

7. stories, poetry, _____

8. great, wonderful, _____

9. never ending, ongoing, _____

10. being, life, _____

11. tamed, cultured, _____

12. provided, supplied, _____

13. tasty, delightful, _____

14. desire, aim, _____

15. name, handwriting, _____

16. enough, plenty, _____

17. clear, easily seen, _____

18. one, not plural, _____

19. fighting, opposition, _____

20. famous, respected, _____

Spelling Words

improvise civilized distinct similar singular
sincerely signature literature committee ambition
assistance resistance existence equipped equipment
sufficient magnificent distinguished
delicious continuous

F. Words and Meanings Write a spelling word for each meaning. Then read down each column to find two more spelling words.

1. to create without preparation

2. of one person or thing

3. a person's handwritten name

4. ongoing

5. desire or aim

6. enough

7. cultured

8. state of being

9. supplied

10. easily seen or heard

11. a group of people with a task

12. aid

13. opposition

14. gear

15. famous

16. tasty

17. stories, poems, and books

18. honestly

19. Write the two spelling words made by the sets of boxes.

G. Using Other Word Forms Add an ending to each adjective to make it an adverb. Then write this Other Word Form to complete each phrase.

Adjective	Adverb
1. similar	were _____ dressed
2. singular	are arranged _____
3. sufficient	is equipped _____
4. magnificent	was decorated _____
5. delicious	was prepared _____

H. Challenge Words Write the Challenge Word that completes each analogy.

edible	conspicuous	irresistible	dimensions	penicillin

1. offensive is to **repulsive** as **charming** is to _____
2. Jonas Salk is to **polio vaccine** as **Alexander Fleming** is to _____
3. scale is to **weight** as **tape measure** is to _____
4. unseen is to **hidden** as **seen** is to _____
5. rock is to **inedible** as **apple** is to _____

I. Spelling and Writing Write two or more answers to each question. Use as many Spelling Words, Other Word Forms, and Challenge Words as you can. A few words are suggested. Proofread for spelling using one of the Proofreading Tips from the Yellow Pages.

1. What were the results of the student council meeting?
literature   committee   sufficient   improvise   similar   signature

2. What was the guest's reaction to the homemade candy?
sincerely   distinct   delicious   magnificent   ambition   singular

3. In what ways is the new machine better than the old one?
equipment   existence   assistance   resistance
   continuous   equipped

33

A. Pretest and Proofreading

B. Spelling Words and Phrases

1. hedge	to trim the <u>hedge</u>	
2. envy	green with <u>envy</u>	
3. digest	hard to <u>digest</u>	
4. request	a final <u>request</u>	
5. domestic	a <u>domestic</u> chore	
6. attempt	to <u>attempt</u> to climb	
7. affection	<u>affection</u> for my friend	
8. regretting	<u>regretting</u> the action	
9. successful	a <u>successful</u> business	
10. surrender	will never <u>surrender</u>	
11. offend	may <u>offend</u> us	
12. offense	no <u>offense</u> meant	
13. immense	an <u>immense</u> castle	
14. impression	my first <u>impression</u>	
15. possession	most valued <u>possession</u>	
16. procession	led the <u>procession</u>	
17. doubtless	<u>doubtless</u> proof	
18. resemble	to <u>resemble</u> my father	
19. assemble	parts to <u>assemble</u>	
20. remembrance	a <u>remembrance</u> of the trip	

Other Word Forms

> hedges
> envies, envied, envying
> digested, digestion
> requested
> domestically
> attempting
> affect, affectionate
> regret, regretted
> success, successfully
> surrendering
> offended, offensive
> immensely, immenseness
> impress, impressive,
>   impressed
> possess, possessive
> process, processes
> doubt, doubtlessly
> resembling, resemblance
> assembling, assemblies
> remember, remembered

C. Challenge Words and Phrases

1. compressor	thump of a <u>compressor</u>
2. perpetual	<u>perpetual</u> thought
3. techniques	latest <u>techniques</u>
4. superintendent	the building <u>superintendent</u>
5. sediment	layer of <u>sediment</u>

D. Word Riddles Answer each question with a word from the spelling list. Write each word once.

1. What <u>empt</u> is an effort?
2. What <u>tion</u> is fondness?
3. What <u>vy</u> is jealousy?
4. What <u>ful</u> is winning?
5. What <u>sion</u> creates a lasting memory?
6. What <u>sion</u> is a parade?
7. What <u>sion</u> is owned?
8. What <u>edge</u> can be trimmed?
9. What <u>ense</u> is huge?
10. What <u>ense</u> causes anger?
11. What <u>ance</u> is not forgotten?
12. What <u>end</u> insults?
13. What <u>er</u> gives up?
14. What <u>ble</u> looks alike?
15. What <u>ble</u> gathers together?
16. What <u>est</u> asks?
17. What <u>est</u> absorbs food?
18. What <u>less</u> is without question?
19. What <u>tic</u> is homelike?
20. What <u>ing</u> is feeling sorry?

E. Word Detective Find the missing vowels and write the spelling words.

1. r _ q _ _ st
2. _ nv _
3. r _ s _ mbl _
4. _ tt _ mpt
5. s _ rr _ nd _ r
6. r _ m _ mbr _ nc _
7. _ ss _ mbl _
8. _ ff _ ct _ _ n
9. _ mm _ ns _
10. d _ g _ st
11. s _ cc _ ssf _ l
12. _ ff _ ns _
13. r _ gr _ tt _ ng
14. h _ dg _
15. p _ ss _ ss _ _ n
16. _ ff _ nd
17. _ mpr _ ss _ _ n
18. d _ m _ st _ c
19. pr _ c _ ss _ _ n
20. d _ _ btl _ ss

Spelling Words

hedge	*envy*	*digest*	*request*	*domestic*	*attempt*
affection	*regretting*	*successful*	*surrender*	*offend*	
offense	*immense*	*impression*	*possession*	*procession*	
doubtless	*resemble*	*assemble*	*remembrance*		

F. Word Parts Join the word parts in each group to write spelling words.

1.

di	vy
en	quest
re	fense
of	gest

2.

at	fend
of	mense
doubt	tempt
im	less

3.

af	pres	brance
re	fect	sion
im	cess	ion
suc	ses	sion
pos	mem	ful

4.

re	gret	ble
do	mes	der
as	ces	ting
pro	sem	sion
re	ren	tic
sur	sem	ble

5. Write the word that was not used.

G. Using Other Word Forms Write the Other Word Form that completes each series.

1. envies, _____ , envying
2. surrenders, surrendered, _____
3. impresses, _____ , impressing
4. assembles, assembled, _____
5. requests, _____ , requesting

H. Challenge Words Write the Challenge Word that completes each quotation.

compressor	perpetual	techniques	superintendent	sediment

1. Teacher: "The school _____ oversees all educational matters."
2. Geologist: "When the river overflows, _____ is deposited on the land."
3. Aerobics Instructor: "All new exercise _____ must be tested for safety."
4. Scientist: "The ocean is a study in _____ motion."
5. Sanitary Engineer: "All trash is crushed in a _____ ."

I. Spelling and Writing Use each phrase in a sentence. You may want to use the words in a different order or use Other Word Forms. Proofread for spelling using one of the Proofreading Tips from the Yellow Pages.

1. planted the hedge
2. without envy
3. digest the food
4. request a loan
5. a domestic animal
6. attempt to mend
7. our affection for them
8. regretting the move
9. a successful person
10. never surrender
11. tries not to offend
12. each traffic offense
13. an immense country
14. left an impression
15. a personal possession
16. the grand procession
17. is doubtless true
18. does resemble you
19. assemble the troops
20. a lasting remembrance

34

A. Pretest and Proofreading

B. Spelling Words and Phrases

1. **crystal** — ice crystal
2. **physical** — physical exam
3. **syllable** — pronouncing each syllable
4. **sympathy** — expressed their sympathy
5. **ambitious** — ambitious project
6. **voluntary** — voluntary attendance
7. **honorable** — an honorable person
8. **accomplish** — to accomplish the goal
9. **unconscious** — seemed to be unconscious
10. **uncommon** — an uncommon plant
11. **absence** — too long an absence
12. **laboratory** — tested at the laboratory
13. **satisfactory** — a satisfactory job
14. **afford** — can't afford to travel
15. **enormous** — enormous appetite
16. **authority** — acted without authority
17. **majorities** — different majorities
18. **minorities** — spoke for the minorities
19. **historical** — historical monument
20. **unfortunate** — unfortunate event

C. Challenge Words and Phrases

1. **circulatory** — circulatory system
2. **moccasins** — beaded moccasins
3. **profitable** — profitable business
4. **physicist** — ideas of the physicist
5. **sympathetic** — a sympathetic inquiry

Other Word Forms

crystallize
physics, physically
syllables
sympathies, sympathetic
ambition, ambitiously
volunteer, voluntarily
honor, honorably
accomplishes
conscious, unconsciously
common, uncommonly
absent
laboratories
satisfy
affordable
enormity, enormously
authorities, authoritative
major, majority
minor, minority
history
fortune, fortunate,
  unfortunately

D. Context Clues Write a word from the spelling list to complete each sentence.

1. The workers offered to do _____ service for the charity.
2. Everyone could give me _____ , but no one could help me.
3. It was unusual to _____ such a difficult task so quickly.
4. The _____ suddenly shattered into a thousand pieces.
5. The elephant was of _____ size.
6. There's nothing _____ about having two eyes and two ears.
7. The boy fell and became _____ when he hit his head.
8. The hero was awarded a medal for her _____ act of courage.
9. The _____ incident was truly a tragedy.
10. In order to graduate, a student must have _____ grades.
11. Only the mayor is an _____ on that subject.
12. The twins are _____ ; they will be successful in the future.
13. The smaller political parties are _____ .
14. Contribute as much as you can _____ .
15. The _____ of two players caused us to lose the contest.
16. Such _____ labor made me exhausted.
17. All the animals are loose in the science _____ .
18. I enjoy visiting _____ houses, especially those of colonial times.
19. Give me an example of a word with only one _____ .
20. Groups that represent more than half of the people are _____ .

E. Not _____ , But Write the spelling word that best fits each phrase.

1. not mental, but _____
2. not usual, but _____
3. not lucky, but _____
4. not tiny, but _____
5. not aware, but _____
6. not forced, but _____
7. not glass, but _____
8. not fail, but _____
9. not have too little money for, but _____
10. not lazy, but _____
11. not minorities, but _____
12. not presence, but _____
13. not majorities, but _____
14. not a word, but a _____
15. not a beginner, but an _____
16. not disgraceful, but _____
17. not an observatory, but a _____
18. not unacceptable, but _____
19. not futuristic, but _____
20. not rejection, but _____

Spelling Words

> crystal physical syllable sympathy ambitious
> voluntary honorable accomplish unconscious
> uncommon absence laboratory satisfactory
> afford enormous authority majorities minorities
> historical unfortunate

F. Word Search The spelling words and some Other Word Forms (p. 136) can be found in the word puzzle. The words appear across, down, and diagonally. Write the words.

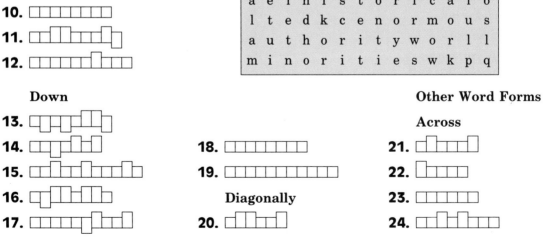

Spelling Words

Across

1.
2.
3.
4.
5.
6.
7.
8.
9.
10.
11.
12.

```
s a t i s f a c t o r y e u
y p r i a m b i t i o u s n
m h i p h y s i c a l a r c
p u h l a b o r a t o r y o
a n c a h o n o r a b l e n
t f z c h a b s e n t n p s
h o f c o a b s e n c e n c
y r s o v o l u n t a r y i
c t y m r h o n o r q u e o
r u l p z d w c l l x o d u
y n l l m a j o r i t i e s
s a a i x c o m m o n o d w
t t b s v t a m b i t i o n
a e l h i s t o r i c a l o
l t e d k c e n o r m o u s
a u t h o r i t y w o r l l
m i n o r i t i e s w k p q
```

Down

13.
14.
15.
16.
17.
18.
19.

Diagonally

20.

Other Word Forms

Across

21.
22.
23.
24.

G. Using Other Word Forms
Add an ending to each adjective to make it an adverb. Then write this Other Word Form to complete each phrase.

Adjective **Adverb**

1. physical _____ handicapped
2. unconscious worked _____
3. ambitious studied _____
4. enormous _____ effective
5. honorable _____ rewarded

H. Challenge Words
Write the Challenge Word that completes each phrase.

circulatory	moccasins	profitable	physicist	sympathetic

1. either the _____ system or digestive system
2. either sandals or _____
3. either compassionate or _____
4. either rewarding or _____
5. either a chemist or a _____

I. Spelling and Writing
Write each set of words in a sentence. You may use Other Word Forms. Proofread your work.

1. unfortunate – honorable – sympathy
2. historical – majorities – minorities
3. ambitious – unconscious – voluntary
4. absence – uncommon – physical
5. syllable – satisfactory – authority
6. laboratory – enormous – accomplish
7. afford – moccasins – crystal
8. circulatory – physically – laboratories
9. sympathetic – profitable – physicist

35

A. Pretest and Proofreading

B. Spelling Words and Phrases

1. mathematics	does well in <u>mathematics</u>	
2. capacity	two-gallon <u>capacity</u>	
3. mechanical	<u>mechanical</u> parts	
4. gigantic	<u>gigantic</u> ship	
5. imagine	hard to <u>imagine</u>	
6. examines	<u>examines</u> closely	
7. recommend	will <u>recommend</u> you	
8. unnecessary	completely <u>unnecessary</u>	
9. poison	<u>poison</u> from the plant	
10. moisten	to <u>moisten</u> the sponge	
11. disappointment	hid my <u>disappointment</u>	
12. summary	<u>summary</u> of the book	
13. boundary	crossing the <u>boundary</u>	
14. announce	will <u>announce</u> the winner	
15. courageous	<u>courageous</u> action	
16. thorough	<u>thorough</u> cleaning	
17. journal	kept a <u>journal</u>	
18. colonel	saluted the <u>colonel</u>	
19. earnest	<u>earnest</u> and thoughtful	
20. rural	<u>rural</u> community	

C. Challenge Words and Phrases

1. **prejudice**   without <u>prejudice</u>
2. **tactics**   unfair <u>tactics</u>
3. **virtually**   <u>virtually</u> abandoned
4. **tragically**   <u>tragically</u> overlooked
5. **versatile**   a <u>versatile</u> dancer

Other Word Forms

mathematical, math
capacities
mechanic
giant
image, imagination
examine, examination
recommended,
   recommendation
necessary, unnecessarily
poisonous
moist, moisture
appoint, disappointed
summaries, summarize
bound, boundaries
announcing, announcement
courage
thoroughly
journalist
colonels
earnestly
rurally

D. All in a Row Write the twenty spelling words in alphabetical order. Then join the boxed letters and write four hidden words.

1. _ _ _ _ _ _☐_

2. _ _ _ _ _ _☐_

3. _ _ _☐_ _ _ _

4. _ _ _ _☐_ _

5. _ _ _ _ _ _☐_ _ _

6. Hidden Word: _____

7. _ _ _ _☐_ _ _ _ _ _ _

8. _ _☐_ _ _ _ _

9. _ _ _ _☐_ _ _

10. _ _ _ _☐_ _☐

11. _ _ _ _ _ _☐

12. Hidden Word: _____

13. _ _ _ _ _ _☐

14. _☐_ _ _ _ _☐_ _ _

15. _ _☐☐_ _ _ _ _ _

16. _ _ _ _ _ _☐_

17. _ _ _☐_ _

18. Hidden Word: _____

19. _ _☐_ _ _ _ _ _

20. _ _ _☐_

21. _ _ _ _ _ _☐_

22. _ _ _☐_ _ _ _

23. _ _ _ _ _ _ _ _ _ _☐

24. Hidden Word: _____

E. Complete the Equations Write the spelling words to complete the equations. You may wish to check the meanings of *boundary* and *capacity* in the **Spelling Dictionary**.

1. diary =

2. suggest =

3. dry ≠

4. sincere =

5. medicine ≠

6. shortened form =

7. volume =

8. urban ≠

9. brave =

10. complete =

11. captain ≠

12. arithmetic =

13. required ≠

14. by hand ≠

15. declare =

16. pretend =

17. limit =

18. success ≠

19. studies =

20. tiny ≠

Spelling Words

> *mathematics capacity mechanical gigantic imagine*
> *examines recommend unnecessary poison moisten*
> *disappointment summary boundary announce*
> *courageous thorough journal colonel earnest rural*

F. Guide Words These word pairs are guide words that might appear in a dictionary. Write the words from the spelling list that would appear on the same page as each pair of guide words.

alley – attempt
1. ____

attitude – bullies
2. ____

bullpen – circumference
3. ____

civil – compare
4. ____

continuous – define
5. ____

definition – disturbance
6. ____

domestic – equip
7. ____

equipment – extreme
8. ____

generate – harried
9. ____

harry – incident
10. ____

indicate – joy
11. ____

linger – memorable
12. ____   13. ____

memorial – neglect
14. ____

plentiful – proceed
15. ____

quality – remember
16. ____

remembrance – scaling
17. ____

slumber – summon
18. ____

suppose – uncommon
19. ____

unconscious – voluntary
20. ____

G. Using Other Word Forms Write the Other Word Form that completes each sentence.

1. An _____ (examines) is a formal test.
2. The word _____ (unnecessary) means not essentially.
3. To _____ (summary) is to restate briefly.
4. A _____ (poison) substance can be deadly.
5. The _____ (boundary) of his land are marked by fences.

H. Challenge Words Write the Challenge Word that completes each question.

prejudice	tactics	virtually	tragically	versatile

1. How did you know the performer was so talented and _____ ?
2. Why did the movie have to end so _____ ?
3. When will they devise new _____ to overcome acid rain?
4. Will they resolve the problem without _____ ?
5. How do you start over when you have lost _____ everything in a flood?

I. Spelling and Writing Write *two* or more answers to each question. Use as many Spelling Words, Other Word Forms, and Challenge Words as you can. A few words are suggested. Proofread your work.

1. What would you do if you had to reach a great many people in your neighborhood with a very important message?

   gigantic – mechanical – moisten – rural – tactics – announce

2. What would you say in a report about your feelings if you had traveled to a deserted planet that appeared to have once been inhabited?

   examines – recommend – summary – boundary – tragically – virtually

3. If you had a problem in school one day, how would you tell your family about it?

   earnest – versatile – unnecessary – disappointment – courageous – journal

REVIEWING LESSONS 31-35

ambitious	composition	earnest	omission	resistance
ammunition	continuous	equipment	position	similar
authority	description	immense	procession	singular
capacity	distinct	improvise	regretting	syllable
civilized	doubtless	majorities	religion	vicinity

A. Bases and Other Word Forms

Write the base words for each spelling word. Then write an Other Word Form. If you need help, use the **Spelling Dictionary**.

Example: description _describe_ _described_

1. omission

2. composition

3. majorities

4. civilized

5. singular

6. resistance

7. equipment

8. continuous

9. regretting

10. procession

11. doubtless

12. ambitious

Write an Other Word Form for each spelling word. If you need help, use the **Spelling Dictionary**.

13. vicinity

14. ammunition

15. religion

16. improvise

17. distinct

18. similar

19. immense

20. syllable

21. authority

22. capacity

23. earnest

24. position

■ courageous	★ assistance	▲ disappointment	♦ surrender	● attempt
mathematics	enormous	request	impression	historical
journal	imagine	gigantic	recommend	opinion
successful	disposition	assemble	absence	captivity
physical	rural	thorough	particularly	equipped

B. Either-Or Write Other Word Forms or the spelling words to complete the phrases. If you need help, use the **Spelling Dictionary**.

1. either defended ■ _____ or ♦ _____ cowardly

2. either ★ _____ by a friend or ● _____ on your own

3. either very ▲ _____ or greatly ♦ _____

4. either ■ _____ correct or ● _____ true

5. either ♦ _____ in person or ▲ _____ in writing

6. either ★ _____ large or ▲ _____ huge

7. either writing in your ■ _____ or ★ _____ adventures in your mind.

8. either having ● _____ or showing an ♦ _____ mind

9. either finding ■ _____ in escaping or remaining a ● _____

10. either easily ▲ _____ or ♦ _____ difficult to connect

11. either having a poor ★ _____ or being ■ _____ tired

12. either fully ● _____ or ▲ _____ unprepared

13. either residing in the city or living in a ★ _____ area

affection	crystal	literacy	possession	sincerely
afford	delicious	mechanical	possibilities	summary
ambition	envy	minorities	refrigerate	sympathy
announce	examines	moisten	remembrance	unfortunate
anticipate	hedge	offend	resemble	unnecessary

C. Word Clues Write the spelling word that best fits each word clue. Then write an Other Word Form for each spelling word. If you need help, use the **Spelling Dictionary**.

1. to keep cool
2. to think about in advance
3. an aim or drive
4. the ability to read
5. the smaller groups
6. unlucky
7. operated by a machine
8. quartz
9. a feeling of pity
10. to dampen
11. to insult
12. ownership
13. tasty
14. a feeling of fondness
15. a dense row of shrubs
16. to have enough money for
17. looks at closely
18. a souvenir
19. a shortened version
20. things that could happen
21. truly
22. to resent
23. to be like
24. to give notice of
25. not needed

R
E
V
I
E
W

accomplish	condition	domestic	magnificent	signature
boundary	decision	existence	offense	sufficient
colonel	definition	honorable	pigeon	uncommon
commission	digest	laboratory	poison	unconscious
committee	distinguished	literature	satisfactory	voluntary

D. Two Extra Remove the two extra letters in each nonsense word. Write the remaining letters in order to complete the phrases with Other Word Forms of the spelling words. If you need help, use the **Spelling Dictionary**.

1. esuffwiciently   _____ supplied
2. ciommitxtees   two new budget _____
3. volusnteaer   may _____ your services
4. toffenseas   apologized for the many _____
5. hboundarides   within the _____
6. defminitionws   checked both _____
7. magtnificenzce   the _____ of a sunrise
8. dicgestked   _____ the meal before running
9. coimmirssions   two _____ on energy
10. existen   need oxygen to _____
11. uncownscirously   _____ made an error
12. poiqsonouus   a _____ snake
13. swatisdfactorily   performed _____
14. literacuye   a _____ test
15. pigdepons   many homing _____
16. bcolmonels   generals and _____
17. acccomvplished   _____ the task
18. crondeitions   some _____ of the game
19. łabroratorieks   science _____
20. pdomedstically   _____ made
21. distingruishinog   several _____ features
22. honorbe   an act of _____
23. deacisiond   a final _____
24. siwgnaturzes   wrote our _____
25. undcomrmonly   _____ chosen as a career

R
E
V
I
E
W

Your Spelling Dictionary/WORDFINDER lists all the basic spelling words and Other Word Forms in your spelling book. If the entry word is a spelling word, it is listed in **dark type**. If the entry word is not in dark type, then the spelling word is listed with the Other Word Forms at the end of the definition.

The Spelling Dictionary/WORDFINDER gives you a quick way to check the spelling and meanings of your spelling words. Because the Spelling Dictionary/WORDFINDER includes many of the words you will need in daily writing, you will find it useful for other schoolwork too.

Sample entries ——

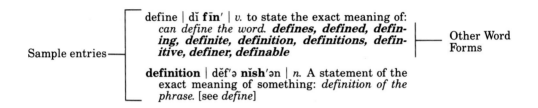

define | dĭ **fīn'** | v. to state the exact meaning of: *can define the word.* **defines, defined, defining, definite, definition, definitions, definitive, definer, definable** —— Other Word Forms

definition | dĕf'ə **nĭsh'ən** | n. A statement of the exact meaning of something: *definition of the phrase.* [see *define*]

PRONUNCIATION KEY

ă	pat	j	judge	sh	dish, ship
ā	aid, fey, pay	k	cat, kick, pique	t	tight
â	air, care, wear	l	lid, needle	th	path, thin
ä	father	m	am, man, mum	th	bathe, this
b	bib	n	no, sudden	ŭ	cut, rough
ch	church	ng	thing	û	circle, firm, heard,
d	deed	ŏ	horrible, pot		term, turn, urge, word
ĕ	pet, pleasure	ō	go, hoarse, row, toe	v	cave, valve, vine
ē	be, bee, easy, leisure	ô	alter, caught, for, paw	w	with
f	fast, fife, off, phase, rough	oi	boy, noise, oil	y	yes
g	gag	ou	cow, out	yōo	abuse, use
h	hat	ŏŏ	took	z	rose, size, xylophone, zebra
hw	which	ōo	boot, fruit	zh	garage, pleasure, vision
ĭ	pit	p	pop	ə	about, silent, pencil
ī	by, guy, pie	r	roar		lemon, circus
î	dear, deer, fierce, mere	s	miss, sauce, see	ər	butter

STRESS
Primary stress ´ **bi•ol´o•gy** |bī **ŏl'** ə jē| Secondary stress   **bi´o•log´i•cal** |bī´ə **lŏj'** ĭ kəl|

©1977 by Houghton Mifflin Company. Reprinted by permission from THE AMERICAN HERITAGE SCHOOL DICTIONARY.

A

able | ā′bəl | *adj.* Having the power, ability, or means to accomplish something: *able to ski well.* **abler, ablest, ably, ability**

ablest | ā′blĭst | *adj.* Having the most power, ability, or means to accomplish something: *the ablest student.* [see *able*]

absence | ăb′səns | *n.* The period of time during which one is not present: *an absence of two weeks.* [see *absent*]

absent | ăb′sənt | *adj.* Not present: *absent from class.* **absence, absences, absentee, absenteeism, absently**

absolute | ăb′sə lōōt′ | *adj.* Total: *absolute freedom.* **absolutely, absoluteness**

abstract | ăb′străkt′ | *adj.* **1.** Hard to understand: *an abstract answer.* **2.** In art, relating to designs that do not represent anything: *abstract pattern.* **abstracts, abstractly, abstractness**

accompany | ə kŭm′pə nē | *v.* To go with: *will accompany you to the movie.* **accompanies, accompanied, accompanying, accompaniment, accompanist**

accomplish | ə kŏm′plĭsh | *v.* To complete; do: *will accomplish the task.* **accomplishes, accomplished, accomplishing, accomplishment**

accurate | ăk′yər ĭt | *adj.* Correct; precise: *accurate health records.* **accurately, accuracy, accurateness**

accuse | ə kyōōz′ | *v.* To blame someone for something done wrong: *won't accuse the student of cheating.* **accuses, accused, accusing, accusingly, accuser, accusation**

accustom | ə kŭs′təm | *v.* To get someone or oneself used to: *will accustom myself to hot weather.* **accustoms, accustomed, accustoming**

accustomed | ə kŭs′təmd | *adj.* Customary; usual: *the accustomed response.* **—Accustomed to—** Used to. [see *accustom*]

acquaint | ə kwānt′ | *v.* **1.** To make oneself known: *to acquaint myself with them.* **2.** To make aware; inform: *will acquaint you with your job.* **acquaints, acquainted, acquainting, acquaintance, acquaintances**

acquaintance | ə kwān′təns | *n.* A person known slightly: *a mere acquaintance.* [see *acquaint*]

acquire | ə kwīr′ | *v.* To obtain; gain: *might acquire a new house.* **acquires, acquired, acquiring**

acquired | ə kwīrd′ | *v.* Obtained; gained: *had acquired an education.* [see *acquire*]

adapt | ə dăpt′ | *v.* To adjust to a specified use or situation: *adapt the novel for television.* **adapts, adapted, adapting, adaptive, adaptable, adapter, adaptation**

adapted | ə dăp′tĭd | *v.* Adjusted to a specified situation: *adapted to the environment.* [see *adapt*]

administer | ăd mĭn′ĭ stər | *v.* To direct or manage: *will administer the office.* **administers, administered, administering, administrate, administrative, administration, administrations, administrator**

administration | ăd mĭn′ĭ strā′shən | *adj.* Relating to the act of directing or managing: *administration building.* *n.* **1.** The officials who direct or manage something: *the college administration.* **2.** Time in office: *the president's administration.* [see *administer*]

affair | ə fâr′ | *n.* **1.** A job or task: *an important affair for the senator.* **2.** A formal occasion: *a black-tie affair.* **affairs**

affect | ə fĕkt′ | *v.* To influence the emotions of: *when songs affect my mood.* **affects, affected, affecting, affection, affections, affectionate, affectionately**

affection | ə fĕk′shən | *n.* A feeling of fondness: *feel affection for my aunt.* [see *affect*]

afford | ə fôrd′ | *v.* To be capable of paying for: *can afford a new pair of skis.* **affords, afforded, affording, affordable**

agency | ā′jən sē | *n.* A business or a service that acts for others: *a ticket agency.* [see *agent*]

agent | ā′jənt | *n.* A representative; someone with the power of authority to act for someone else: *an insurance agent.* **agents, agency, agencies**

agree | ə grē′ | *v.* **1.** To grant consent: *agree to do the work.* **2.** To come to an understanding: *agree on a course of action.* **agrees, agreed, agreeing, agreeable, disagree, disagreeable**

agricultural | ăg′rĭ kŭl′ chər əl | *adj.* Related to farming: *new agricultural methods.* [see *agriculture*]

agriculture | ăg′rĭ kŭl′ chər | *n.* Farming: *a career in agriculture.* **agricultural, agriculturally, agriculturalist**

aisle | īl | *n.* A pathway between rows of seats in a classroom, theater, etc.: *a wide aisle.* **aisles**

alley | ăl′ē | *n.* A narrow street or passage between buildings: *walked through the alley.* **alleys**

ambition | ăm bĭsh′ən | *n.* A very strong desire to achieve something: *had ambition to win.* **ambitions, ambitionless, ambitious, ambitiously**

ambitious | ăm bĭsh′əs | *adj.* **1.** Having high goals; far-reaching: *ambitious plan.* **2.** Eager to succeed: *ambitious student.* [see *ambition*]

ambulance | ăm′byə ləns | *n.* A vehicle equipped to rush people to a hospital: *pulled over until the ambulance passed.* [see *ambulate*]

ambulate | ăm′byə lāt′ | *v.* To walk: *will ambulate slowly to school.* **ambulates, ambulated, ambulating, ambulation, ambulatory, ambulance, ambulances**

ammunition | ăm′yə nĭsh′ən | *n.* Anything that can be fired from a gun: *no more ammunition.* **ammunitions**

analyze | ăn′ə līz′ | *v.* To study in detail: *will analyze the data.* **analyzes, analyzed, analyzing, analytic, analytical, analysis, analyst**

ancestor | ăn′sĕs′tər | *n.* A person from whom someone is descended; a forefather: *an ancestor of this person.* **ancestors, ancestral, ancestry**

anchor | ăng′kər | *n.* A heavy piece of metal lowered by a rope to fix a boat in a specific place in the water: *drop the anchor in the bay.* **anchors, anchored, anchoring, anchorage**

ancient | ān′shənt | *adj.* Very old; aged: *an ancient civilization.* **ancients, ancientness**

animate | ăn′ə māt′ | *v.* **1.** To make lively and energetic: *animate the quiet party.* **2.** To produce as a cartoon, with figures moving: *will animate a cat fight for the cartoon.* **animates, animated, animating, animation, animatedly, animator**

animated | ăn′ə mā′tĭd | *adj.* **1.** Filled with life; lively: *an animated debate.* **2.** Made to seem alive: *an animated cartoon.* [see *animate*]

anniversary | ăn′ə vûr′sə rē | *n.* The yearly return of the date of an event that happened in a previous year: *celebrated the anniversary of our meeting.* **anniversaries**

announce | ə nouns′ | *v.* To declare publicly: *will announce the results.* **announces, announced, announcing, announcement, announcer**

annual | ăn′yoō əl | *adj.* Yearly; once a year: *the annual event.* **annuals, annually**

anticipate | ăn tĭs′ə pāt′ | *v.* To foresee or think about in advance: *to anticipate the questions.* **anticipates, anticipated, anticipating, anticipation**

apologize | ə pŏl′ə jīz′ | *v.* To say that one is sorry: *will apologize for the accident.* [see *apology*]

appetite | ăp′ĭ tīt′ | *n.* The desire to eat: *had an appetite.* **appetites, appetize, appetizer**

apply | ə plī′ | *v.* **1.** To ask for: *apply for a position.* **2.** To spread on: *apply glue to the frame.* **applies, applied, applying, application, applicant, applicable, applicator**

appoint | ə point′ | *v.* To choose for an office or position: *will appoint her as judge.* **disappoint, disappoints, disappointed, disappointing, disappointment, disappointments**

appreciate | ə prē′shē āt′ | *v.* To recognize the worth of: *can appreciate friends.* **appreciates, appreciated, appreciating, appreciable, appreciably, appreciative, appreciation**

approach | ə prōch′ | *n.* Method: *a practical approach.* *v.* To come nearer: *will approach the stage.* **approaches, approached, approaching, approachable**

artificial | är′tə fĭsh′əl | *adj.* Not natural; made by human skill or labor: *artificial plants.* **artificially, artificialness**

aside | ə sīd′ | *adv.* To one side: *has put the work aside.* **asides**

assemble | ə sĕm′bəl | *v.* **1.** To put together: *assemble the model.* **2.** To gather together: *assemble a group.* **assembles, assembled, assembling, assembly, assemblies**

assist | ə sĭst′ | *v.* To give aid; help: *will assist the waitress.* **assists, assisted, assisting, assistance, assistant**

assistance | ə sĭs′təns | *n.* The act of helping: *gave assistance to the child.* [see *assist*]

associate | ə sō′sē āt′ | *v.* To join in a group as a member: *will associate with the law firm.* **associates, associated, associating, association, associations**

association | ə sō′sē ā′shən | *n.* A society; a group of people who have joined together: *an association to help needy students.* [see *associate*]

assure | ə shoŏr′ | *v.* To guarantee: *will assure victory.* **assures, assured, assuring, assuredly, assurance**

ă pat / ā pay / â care / ä father / ĕ pet / ē be / ĭ pit / ī pie / î fierce / ŏ pot / ō go / ô paw, for / oi oil / oŏ book / oō boot / ou out / ŭ cut / û fur / *th* the / th thin / hw which / zh vision / ə ago, item, pencil, atom, circus
©1977 by Houghton Mifflin Company. Reprinted by permission from THE AMERICAN HERITAGE SCHOOL DICTIONARY.

attempt | ə **tĕmpt'** | v. To try: *will attempt to sail the boat.* n. An effort: *an attempt to finish the race.* **attempts, attempted, attempting**

attitude | **ăt'ĭ tōōd'** | n. A person's feeling toward someone or something, often shown by behavior: *a good attitude toward studying.* **attitudes**

authority | ə **thôr'ĭ tē** | n. 1. The right and power to do something: *has the authority to cancel.* 2. An expert: *a government authority.* **authorities, authoritative, authoritarian, authorize, authorization**

automate | **ô'tə māt'** | v. To make automatic or operable without human control: *to automate the washing of dishes.* **automates, automated, automating, automatic, automation**

automation | **ô'tə mā'shən** | n. A machine-operated system or process: *automation of the car industry.* [see *automate*]

avail | ə **vāl'** | v. To be of use to: *if aid will avail you.* **avails, availed, availing, available, availably, availableness, availability**

available | ə **vā'lə bəl** | adj. Able to be obtained: *all the available information.* [see *avail*]

aviate | **ā'vē āt'** | v. To fly a plane: *aviate the jet.* **aviates, aviated, aviating, aviator, aviation**

aviation | **ā'vē ā'shən** | adj. Relating to the operation of an aircraft: *an aviation student.* n. The operation of an aircraft: *careful aviation of the plane.* [see *aviate*]

await | ə **wāt'** | v. To wait for; expect: *will await your decision.* **awaits, awaited, awaiting**

B

bacteria | **băk tîr'ē ə** | n. Any of several microscopic organisms existing as free-living organisms or as parasites: *a culture of bacteria.* **bacterium**

ballet | **bă lā'** | n. A dance performed in costume and to music, with precise and graceful turns, jumps, etc.: *a classical ballet.* **ballets, ballerina**

ballot | **băl'ət** | n. The paper on which a vote is recorded in an election: *secret ballot for president.* **ballots, balloted, balloting**

banister | **băn'ĭ stər** | n. The handrail supported by posts along some stairs: *held the banister.* **banisters**

banquet | **băng'kwĭt** | n. A feast; an elaborate meal: *planned a banquet for 20 people.* **banquets, banqueted, banqueting**

benefit | **bĕn'ə fĭt** | v. To provide help to; be beneficial to: *benefit his ability to learn.* n. An advantage: *a benefit in practicing.* **benefits, benefited, benefiting, beneficial, beneficiary**

benefits | **bĕn'ə fĭts** | v. Provides help to; is beneficial to: *if the law benefits society.* n. Advantages: *gain benefits from a good diet.* [see *benefit*]

bestow | **bĭ stō'** | v. To give or present: *will bestow an award.* **bestows, bestowed, bestowing, bestowal**

birth | **bûrth** | n. The act of becoming alive; the beginning of a person's life: *the birth of her daughter.* **births, birthed, birthing**

biscuit | **bĭs'kĭt** | n. A type of bread, similar to a roll, made with baking powder, baking soda, or yeast: *strawberries on top of a biscuit.* **biscuits**

biweekly | **bī wēk'lē** | adj. Happening every two weeks: *prepared the biweekly report.* [see *week*]

blanket | **blăng'kĭt** | v. To cover or obscure: *will blanket the issue.* **blankets, blanketed, blanketing**

blanketed | **blăng'kĭ tĭd** | adj. Covered: *blanketed with soft snow.* [see *blanket*]

bluff | **blŭf** | v. To mislead by a false show of confidence: *will bluff through the discussion.* **bluffs, bluffed, bluffing, bluffer**

bluffed | **blŭft** | v. Misled by a false show of confidence: *bluffed during the game.* [see *bluff*]

boulevard | **bōōl'ə värd'** | n. A wide city street: *turned left on the boulevard.* **boulevards**

bound | **bound** | v. To limit or form the boundary of: *two cities bound a lake.* **bounds, bounded, bounding, boundless, boundary, boundaries**

boundary | **boun'də rē** | n. A dividing line or edge of something such as a country, state, etc.: *boundary between the U.S. and Canada.* [see *bound*]

briar | **brī'ər** | adj. Of a briar: *briar bushes.* n. A thorny bush: *briar in the field.* **briars**

brilliance | **brĭl'yəns** | n. Brightness: *a flame's brilliance.* **brilliant, brilliantly**

brilliant | **brĭl'yənt** | adj. Brightly shining: *brilliant sunset.* [see *brilliance*]

bullies | **bōōl'ēz** | n. More than one bully: *avoided the bullies on the corner.* [see *bully*]

bullpen | **bōōl'pĕn'** | n. The area in a baseball stadium where pitchers warm up: *practiced the pitch in the bullpen.* **bullpens**

bully | **bŏŏl′**ē | *n.* A tough, quarrelsome person who picks on weaker people: *won't listen to the bully.* **bullies, bullied, bullying**

bump | bŭmp | *v.* To knock against someone or something: *bump into me.* **bumps, bumped, bumping, bumper, bumpers, bumpy**

bumper | **bŭm′**pər | *n.* A metal or rubber bar attached to the front and rear of a car to absorb shock in a collision: *polished the rusty bumper.* [see *bump*]

C

campaign | kăm **pān′** | *n.* A planned course of activities for a special purpose: *the senator's campaign.* *v.* To run for office: *will campaign for governor.* **campaigns, campaigned, campaigning, campaigner**

candidate | **kăn′**dĭ dāt′ | *n.* A person running for an office: *if our candidate wins.* **candidates, candidacy**

canoe | kə **nōō′** | *n.* A boat with pointed ends, moved by paddles: *the canoe in the river.* **canoes, canoed, canoeing, canoeist**

capacity | kə **păs′**ĭ tē | *n.* The ability to hold; volume: *a capacity of eleven gallons.* **capacities**

captive | **kăp′**tĭv | *n.* A person or an animal held prisoner: *when the criminal was a captive.* **captives, captivity, captor, capture**

captivity | kăp **tĭv′**ĭ tē | *n.* The period of time or the state of being a prisoner: *kept in captivity.* [see *captive*]

carbon | **kär′**bən | *n.* A sheet of paper coated on one side with a dark color, used between sheets of writing paper to make copies: *traced with a carbon.* **–Carbon copy–** A duplicate of anything written or typed, made by using carbon paper. **carbons**

career | kə **rîr′** | *n.* A profession or occupation: *successful acting career.* **careers**

carnival | **kär′**nə vəl | *n.* **1.** A place of amusement with outdoor shows and games: *went to the carnival.* **2.** Any festival: *a yearly carnival.* **carnivals**

castaway | **kăst′**ə wā′ | *n.* A person who has been shipwrecked: *save the castaway.* **castaways**

caution | **kô′**shən | *n.* Great carefulness; unwillingness to do risky things: *moved with caution across the footbridge.* **cautions, cautioned, cautioning, cautious, cautiously, cautiousness, cautionary**

cautiously | **kô′**shəs lē | *adj.* Using great care; carefully: *walked cautiously.* [see *caution*]

ceiling | **sē′** lĭng | *n.* The surface of a room opposite the floor: *a high ceiling.* **ceilings**

celebrate | **sĕl′**ə brāt′ | *v.* To mark a special occasion with festivities and parties: *will celebrate her birthday.* **celebrates, celebrated, celebrating, celebration, celebrant, celebrity**

cemetery | **sĕm′**ĭ tĕr′ē | *n.* A place for burying the dead: *will visit the cemetery.* **cemeteries**

centimeter | **sĕn′**tə mē′tər | *n.* A unit of length that is equal to 1/100 of a meter: *measured one centimeter in length.* **centimeters**

cereal | **sîr′**ē əl | *n.* The seeds of wheat, oats, corn, etc., prepared as a food: *breakfast cereal.* **cereals**

ceremony | **sĕr′**ə mō′ nē | *n.* Formal act prescribed by ritual, protocol, or custom: *the marriage ceremony.* **ceremonies, ceremonial**

certificate | sər **tĭf′**ĭ kĭt | *n.* An official document that gives information about a person or thing: *a birth certificate.* [see *certify*]

certify | **sûr′**tə fī | *v.* To conform or to guarantee as true: *will certify the document.* **certifies, certified, certifying, certificate, certificates, certification**

chairperson | **châr′**pûr′sən | *n.* A person in charge of a meeting: *when the chairperson begins the debate.* **chairpersons**

character | **kăr′**ĭk tər | *n.* **1.** A person in a story, novel, play, etc.: *the character in the movie.* **2.** The moral nature of someone; reputation: *has good character.* **characters, characterize, characterization, characteristic**

chorus | **kôr′**əs | *n.* A group of singers who perform with each other: *listened to the chorus.* **choruses, chorused, chorusing, choral**

circulate | **sûr′**kyə lāt′ | *v.* **1.** To move or cause to move around in an area: *may circulate fresh air.* **2.** To send from place to place: *to circulate information.* **circulates, circulated, circulating, circulatory, circulator, circulation**

ă pat / ā pay / â care / ä father / ĕ pet / ē be / ĭ pit / ī pie / î fierce / ŏ pot / ō go / ô paw, for / oi oil / ŏŏ book / ōō boot / ou out / ŭ cut / û fur / th the / th thin / hw which / zh vision / ə ago, item, pencil, atom, circus
©1977 by Houghton Mifflin Company. Reprinted by permission from THE AMERICAN HERITAGE SCHOOL DICTIONARY.

circulation | sûr′kyə lā′shən | *n.* **1.** The act of circulating or causing to move around: *circulation of heat.* **2.** The amount of copies of books, newspapers, etc., sent out at a certain time: *a magazine's circulation.* [see *circulate*]

circumference | sər kŭm′fər əns | *n.* The boundary line of a circle: *the circumference of the wheel.* **circumferential**

civil | sĭv′əl | *adj.* **1.** Polite; with courtesy: *a very civil reply.* **2.** Relating to citizens: *civil rights in America.* **civilly, civilian, civilians, civilize, civilizes, civilized, civilizing, civilization, civilizations**

civilization | sĭv′ə lĭ zā′shən | *n.* A complex society developed by a group of people: *civilization of ancient Egypt.* [see *civil*]

civilized | sĭv′ə līzd′ | *adj.* **1.** Polite and refined: *a civilized act.* **2.** Indicating a developed culture: *civilized ideals.* [see *civil*]

class | klăs | *n.* A group of things or persons with some similarity: *a class of animals.* **classes, classed, classical, classifier, classify, classifies, classified, classifying, classification**

classify | klăs′ə fī′ | *v.* To put into classes or groups: *will classify the cloth by color.* [see *class*]

climax | klī′măks′ | *n.* The most exciting part; the concluding part: *the climax of the movie.* **climaxes, climaxed, climaxing, climactic**

colonel | kûr′nəl | *n.* A U.S. Army, Air Force, or Marine Corps officer, ranking below a brigadier general: *colonel in the Air Force.* **colonels**

column | kŏl′əm | *n.* **1.** A support or pillar shaped like a cylinder: *a house with two columns.* **2.** A regular article in a newspaper or magazine: *a weekly column.* **columns, columned, columnist, columnists**

columnist | kŏl′əm nĭst | *n.* A writer of a regular article, or column, for a paper or magazine: *a political columnist.* [see *column*]

combination | kŏm′bə nā′shən | *n.* **1.** The act of merging; a mixture: *a combination of ingredients.* **2.** A sequence of numbers used to open a lock: *the safe's combination.* [see *combine*]

combine | kəm bīn′ | *v.* To join, merge, or blend: *combine their talents.* **combines, combined, combining, combination**

comet | kŏm′ĭt | *n.* A heavenly body with a star-like head and a glowing tail: *saw the comet through the telescope.* **comets**

comfort | kŭm′fərt | *n.* Anything that makes pain, sorrow, or difficulty easier to bear: *offered comfort to the sick puppy.* **uncomfortable, uncomfortably**

commerce | kŏm′ərs | *n.* Business; trade: *engaged in commerce.* **commercial, commercials, commercially, commercialism, commercialize, commercialization**

commercial | kə mûr′shəl | *n.* A radio or television advertisement: *a commercial for a new product.* [see *commerce*]

commission | kə mĭsh′ən | *n.* An organization or group which has authority to perform certain duties: *commission on safety.* [see *commit*]

commit | kə mĭt′ | *v.* **1.** To do: *to commit a robbery.* **2.** To pledge oneself to a task, position, etc.: *will commit herself to care for the cat.* **commits, committed, committing, commitment, committee, committees, commission, commissions, commissioned, commissioning, commissioner**

committee | kə mĭt′ē | *n.* A group of people who perform specific tasks or duties: *the clean-up committee.* [see *commit*]

common | kŏm′ən | *adj.* Usual; found in many places: *a common insect.* **uncommon, uncommonly, uncommonness**

communicate | kə myoo′nĭ kāt′ | *v.* To make known; exchange ideas, plans, etc.: *communicate the strategy.* **communicates, communicated, communicating, communication, communications, communicator**

communication | kə myoo′nĭ kā′shən | *adj.* Related to communication: *a communication problem.* *n.* The act of exchanging thoughts or information: *frequent communication.* [see *communicate*]

communities | kə myoo′nĭ tēz | *n.* **1.** More than one group of people living together: *several communities working together.* **2.** More than one town: *saw many communities.* [see *community*]

community | kə myoo′nĭ tē | *n.* **1.** A group of people living in the same area: *a rural community.* **2.** A district in which a group of people live; town: *a safe community.* **communities**

commute | kə myoot′ | *v.* To travel daily, as from the suburbs to the city: *commute to work.* **commutes, commuted, commuting, commuter**

commuter | kə myoo′tər | *n.* A person who travels regularly from one place to another: *a commuter to and from work.* [see *commute*]

comparatively | kəm păr′ə tĭv lē | *adv.* By comparison; in relation to others, or relatively: *comparatively joyful.* [see *compare*]

compare | kəm **pâr'** | v. To describe one thing as related to another; point out the similarities between: *will compare a dog to a cat.* **compares, compared, comparing, comparable, comparative, comparatively, comparison**

compete | kəm **pēt'** | v. To take part in a contest; strive against another or others: *will compete in the tournament.* **competes, competed, competing, competitive, competitively, competitiveness, competition, competitor**

compose | kəm **pōz'** | v. To create something such as a story, poem, song, etc.: *can compose music.* **composes, composed, composing, composite, composer, composition, compositions**

composition | kŏm'pə **zĭsh'**ən | n. An essay, short story, etc., that is written as a school exercise: *finished the composition.* [see *compose*]

conclude | kən **klood'** | v. 1. To finish: *will conclude the speech.* 2. To decide: *to conclude you weren't guilty.* **concludes, concluded, concluding, conclusion, conclusions, conclusive, conclusively, conclusiveness**

conclusion | kən **kloo'**zhən | n. 1. The end; the closing part: *conclusion of the performance.* 2. A decision based on experience or reasoning: *finally reached a conclusion.* [see *conclude*]

concrete | kŏn'**krēt'** | n. Paving material made of crushed stone, sand, etc.: *used concrete for the driveway.* adj. Quite specific; solid; not abstract or general: *concrete plan to clean the park.* **concretes, concretely, concreteness**

condition | kən **dĭsh'**ən | n. 1. A state of health or good working order: *improved my condition with exercise.* 2. A requirement: *a condition of the job.* **conditions, conditioned, conditioning, conditional, conditionally**

confer | kən **fûr'** | v. To consult together; hold a special meeting to discuss something: *will confer about the plans.* **confers, conferred, conferring, conference, conferences**

conference | kŏn'fər əns | n. A meeting held to discuss something: *conference on human rights.* [see *confer*]

confine | kən **fīn'** | v. 1. To restrict the movement of: *will confine the dog in the kennel.* 2. To put in jail: *will confine the criminal.* **confines, confined, confining, confinement**

confined | kən **fīnd'** | adj. Restricted in movement: *confined in a cage.* v. Put in jail: *confined him in the state prison.* [see *confine*]

confirm | kən **fûrm'** | v. To make certain; make something binding: *will confirm the flight.* **confirms, confirmed, confirming, confirmation**

conquer | kŏng'kər | v. To get control over; get the better of: *can conquer the disease.* **conquers, conquered, conquering, conqueror**

conscious | kŏn'shəs | adj. Able to think, will, and perceive; using the powers of one's mind: *conscious choice.* **unconscious, unconsciously, unconsciousness**

consider | kən **sĭd'**ər | v. To think over or reflect upon: *to consider the plan.* **considers, considered, considering, consideration, considerations, considerable, considerably, considerate, considerately**

considerably | kən **sĭd'**ər ə blē | adv. A great deal; much: *considerably younger.* [see *consider*]

consideration | kən sĭd'ə **rā'**shən | n. 1. A factor to be thought about in making a decision: *an important consideration.* 2. Very thoughtful concern for others: *showed consideration to the new student.* [see *consider*]

constant | kŏn'stənt | adj. Continuous; not stopping: *a constant humming sound.* **constants, constantly, constancy**

constitute | kŏn'stĭ toot' | v. To make up; form: *will constitute a majority.* **constitutes, constituted, constituting, constitution, constitutions, constitutional, constitutionally**

constitution | kŏn'stĭ **too'**shən | n. The laws or principles of an organized group: *the constitution of the small country.* [see *constitute*]

construct | kən **strŭkt'** | v. To build; put up: *will construct a bridge.* **constructs, constructed, constructing, construction, constructions, constructive**

construction | kən **strŭk'**shən | adj. Relating to the act or process of building: *construction company.* n. The act or process of building: *planned the construction of the school.* [see *construct*]

consult | kən **sŭlt'** | v. To seek information or obtain advice: *consult a doctor.* **consults, consulted, consulting, consultation, consultant**

ă pat / ā pay / â care / ä father / ĕ pet / ē be / ĭ pit / ī pie / î fierce / ŏ pot / ō go / ô paw, for / oi oil / oͦo book / oͦo boot / ou out / ŭ cut / û fur / *th* the / th thin / hw which / zh vision / ə ago, item, pencil, atom, circus
©1977 by Houghton Mifflin Company. Reprinted by permission from THE AMERICAN HERITAGE SCHOOL DICTIONARY.

contact | **kŏn′**tăkt′ | *n.* The condition of touching: *caused contact between the two wires. v.* To get in touch with; communicate: *will contact the job applicants.* **contacts, contacted, contacting**

contain | kən **tān′** | *v.* To hold: *to contain an egg.* **contains, contained, containing, containable, containment, container, containers**

container | kən **tā′**nər | *n.* A box, jar, can, etc., used to hold something: *a container for pens and pencils.* [see *contain*]

continue | kən **tĭn′**yŏŏ | *v.* To keep on: *to continue climbing the mountain.* **continues, continued, continuing, continual, continuous, continuously, continuance, continuation**

continuous | kən **tĭn′**yŏŏ əs | *adj.* Persisting without interruption: *continuous rain.* [see *continue*]

contract | kən **trăkt′** | *v.* To agree formally on certain conditions: *will contract to build the cabin.* **contracts, contracted, contracting, contraction, contractor, contractors**

contractor | **kŏn′**trăk′tər | *n.* A professional who agrees to provide materials and labor for constructing houses, office buildings, etc.: *asked the contractor about the wood.* [see *contract*]

contrary | **kŏn′**trĕr′ē | *adj.* Opposite: *contrary belief to mine.* **contrarily, contrariness**

convene | kən **vēn′** | *v.* To assemble; come together: *will convene at the meeting place.* **convenes, convened, convening, convention**

convenience | kən **vēn′**yəns | *n.* **1.** Personal advantage or comfort: *a car for your convenience.* **2.** A device that saves time: *a modern convenience.* **conveniences, convenient, conveniently**

conversation | **kŏn′**vər **sā′**shən | *n.* The act of conversing; a discussion: *conversation with the family.* [see *converse*]

converse | kən **vûrs′** | *v.* To discuss informally: *converse at dinner.* **converses, conversed, conversing, conversation, conversations, conversational, conversationalist, conversely**

copied | **kŏp′**ēd | *v.* Duplicated; reproduced: *copied the story.* [see *copy*]

copy | **kŏp′**ē | *v.* To duplicate; reproduce: *will copy the sentences.* **copies, copied, copying, copier**

cornerstone | **kôr′**nər stōn′ | *n.* **1.** The stone at a corner of the foundation of a building: *a ceremony to place the cornerstone.* **2.** The foundation or basis: *cornerstone of the plan.* **cornerstones**

correspond | kôr′ĭ **spŏnd′** | *v.* To write letters to one another: *will correspond every week.* **corresponds, corresponded, corresponding, correspondence, correspondent**

courage | **kûr′**ĭj | *n.* Bravery: *faces the future with courage.* **courageous, courageously**

courageous | kə **rā′**jəs | *adj.* Showing bravery: *a courageous person.* [see *courage*]

create | krē **āt′** | *v.* To make; bring into existence: *will create a beautiful painting.* **creates, created, creating, creative, creatively, creativeness, creativity, creation, creations, creator**

crystal | **krĭs′**təl | *n.* **1.** A mass of a fixed shape, with angles and flat sides, into which some substances harden: *quartz crystal.* **2.** Highly transparent glass: *a vase of crystal.* **crystals, crystallize**

custom | **kŭs′**təm | *n.* **1.** A habit; something one usually does: *a custom of arriving early.* **2.** A tradition: *a popular custom.* **customs, customary, customize, customizes, customized, customizing, customer**

D

dark | därk | *adj.* Having little or no light: *the dark house.* **darker, darkest, darkish, darkly, darken, darkens, darkened, darkening, darkener, darkness**

darkened | **där′**kənd | *adj.* Dimmed or without light: *darkened sky after sunset.* [see *dark*]

decade | **dĕk′**ād′ | *n.* A ten-year period: *have known her for a decade.* **decades**

deceive | dĭ **sēv′** | *v.* To make someone believe something is true when it is false: *won't deceive them with a lie.* **deceives, deceived, deceiving, deceivingly, deceiver, deceit**

deceived | dĭ **sēvd′** | *adj.* Made to believe something is true when it is false; fooled: *was deceived by the excuse.* [see *deceive*]

decide | dĭ **sīd′** | *v.* To make up one's mind: *decide today.* **decides, decided, deciding, decidable, decider, decision, decisions, decisive**

decimal | **dĕs′**ə məl | *n.* A number written in base 10; a number containing a decimal point: *a decimal fraction.* **decimals**

decision | dĭ **sĭzh′**ən | *n.* A definite conclusion: *made a decision to resign.* [see *decide*]

decorate | **dĕk′**ə rāt | *v.* To adorn or beautify something: *will decorate the room.* **decorates, decorated, decorating, decorator, decorators, decoration, decorative, decoratively**

decorator | dĕk′ə rā′tər | *n.* A person who decorates or adorns: *called a decorator to plan the new room.* [see *decorate*]

define | dĭ fīn′ | *v.* To state the exact meaning of: *can define the word.* **defines, defined, defining, definite, definition, definitions, definitive, definer, definable**

definition | dĕf′ə nĭsh′ən | *n.* A statement of the exact meaning of something: *definition of the phrase.* [see *define*]

delicate | dĕl′ĭ kĭt | *adj.* Fragile: *a delicate plant.* **delicately, delicateness, delicacy**

delicious | dĭ lĭsh′əs | *adj.* Quite pleasing, especially to taste or smell: *a delicious meal.* **deliciously, deliciousness**

democracy | dĭ mŏk′rə sē | *n.* The type of government in which the power belongs to the people, who use elected representatives to act for them: *American democracy.* **democracies, democrat, democrats, democratic, democratically**

deny | dĭ nī′ | *v.* 1. To refuse to give or allow: *will deny passage.* 2. To state that something is untrue: *to deny the charge.* **denies, denied, denying, denial, deniable, denier**

depart | dĭ pärt′ | *v.* To leave; go away: *will depart for the city.* **departs, departed, departing, departure, departures**

departure | dĭ pär′chər | *n.* The act of leaving or going away: *departure of the train.* [see *depart*]

depot | dē′pō | *n.* 1. A transportation station: *waited at the bus depot.* 2. A warehouse; a place to store something: *a grain depot.* **depots**

describe | dĭ skrīb′ | *v.* To give an account in words of someone or something: *will describe the building.* **describes, described, describing, description, descriptions, describable, descriptive, describer**

description | dĭ skrĭp′shən | *n.* An account in words of someone or something: *description of the painting.* [see *describe*]

despair | dĭ spâr′ | *n.* A complete lack of hope: *felt despair after the flood.* **despairs, despaired, despairing, despairingly, despairer, desperate, desperately, desperateness, desperation**

desperate | dĕs′pər ĭt | *adj.* 1. Very bad; hopeless: *desperate conditions.* 2. Reckless because of loss of hope: *a desperate act.* [see *despair*]

destination | dĕs′tə nā′shən | *n.* The place or position to which someone or something is going: *if the destination is Europe.* [see *destine*]

destine | dĕs′tĭn | *v.* To determine the outcome beforehand, as if by some force that cannot be controlled: *to destine myself for success.* **destines, destined, destining, destiny, destination, destinations**

destiny | dĕs′tə nē | *n.* A person's fortune or fate: *the destiny of the young child.* [see *destine*]

determine | dĭ tûr′mĭn | *v.* To find out precisely: *can determine the number of people.* **determines, determined, determining, determinedly, determination, determinate, determinator, determiner, determinism**

detour | dē′tŏŏr′ | *n.* A by-road used temporarily instead of a main route: *a detour around the accident.* **detours, detoured, detouring**

develop | dĭ vĕl′əp | *v.* 1. To bring into being; work out in detail: *will develop a new computer.* 2. To grow: *to develop from a seed.* **develops, developed, developing, developer, development, developmental**

differ | dĭf′ər | *v.* To disagree: *may differ over the color.* **indifferent, indifferently**

digest | dī jĕst′ | *v.* To change food into a form that can be absorbed by the body: *will digest the meal quickly.* **digests, digested, digesting, digestion, digestible, digestive**

dinosaur | dī′nə sôr′ | *adj.* Of a dinosaur: *a dinosaur track.* *n.* A type of reptile, now extinct: *a skeleton of a dinosaur.* **dinosaurs**

diploma | dĭ plō′mə | *n.* A certificate awarded by a school, stating that a course of study has been finished successfully: *earned a diploma from the university.* **diplomas, diplomacy, diplomat**

disagreeable | dĭs′ə grē′ə bəl | *adj.* Unpleasant, offensive: *a disagreeable person.* [see *agree*]

disappointment | dĭs′ə point′mənt | *n.* The feeling of being made unhappy because one's hopes or expectations were frustrated: *felt disappointment at the failure.* [see *appoint*]

disgrace | dĭs grās′ | *n.* Loss of honor; shame: *disgrace after the arrest.* **disgraces, disgraced, disgracing, disgraceful, disgracefully**

displease | dĭs plēz′ | *v.* To offend, disappoint, or annoy: *won't displease my parents.* [see *please*]

ă pat / ā pay / â care / ä father / ĕ pet / ē be / ĭ pit / ī pie / î fierce / ŏ pot / ō go / ô paw, for / oi oil / ŏŏ book / ŏŏ boot / ou out / ŭ cut / û fur / th the / th thin / hw which / zh vision / ə ago, item, pencil, atom, circus
©1977 by Houghton Mifflin Company. Reprinted by permission from THE AMERICAN HERITAGE SCHOOL DICTIONARY.

dispose | dǐ **spōz'** | v. To arrange: *to dispose the glasses in rows.* **–Dispose of–** To get rid of. **disposes, disposed, disposing, disposal, disposable, disposition, dispositions**

disposition | dǐs'pə **zǐsh'**ən | n. A person's usual mood: *a friendly disposition.* [see *dispose*]

distinct | dǐ **stǐngkt'** | adj. Clear; definite: *a distinct photograph.* **distinctly, distinction, distinctive, distinctively, distinctiveness**

distinguish | dǐs **tǐng'**gwǐsh | v. To recognize as being different or distinct: *distinguish each letter in the word.* **distinguishes, distinguished, distinguishing, distinguishable**

distinguished | dǐs **tǐng'**gwǐsht | adj. Characterized by excellence or distinction: *a distinguished author.* [see *distinguish*]

disturb | dǐs **tûrb'** | v. To interrupt or upset: *disturb the animals.* **disturbs, disturbed, disturbing, disturbance**

disturbance | dǐs **tûr'**bəns | n. The act of interrupting or upsetting: *caused a loud disturbance.* [see *disturb*]

domestic | də **měs'**tǐk | adj. Of the home: *a domestic task.* **domestically**

dosage | **dō'**sǐj | n. The amount of medicine given at one time: *a dosage of two vitamins.* [see *dose*]

dose | dōs | n. The amount of medicine given at one time: *a dose of medicine twice daily.* **doses, dosage, dosages**

doubt | dout | n. Uncertainty: *had much doubt.* **doubts, doubted, doubting, doubtful, doubtfully, doubtless, doubtlessly**

doubtless | **dout'**lǐs | adj. Without question; certain: *doubtless evidence.* [see *doubt*]

E

earnest | **ûr'**nǐst | adj. Showing sincerity; serious and purposeful: *earnest and careful.* **earnestly, earnestness**

ease | ēz | n. Freedom from effort: *completed the exam with ease.* **eases, eased, easing, easy, easier, easiest, easily**

easily | **ē'**zə lē | adv. Readily or with little effort: *easily frustrated by the problem.* [see *ease*]

economy | ǐ **kǒn'**ə mē | n. The management of resources: *economy of the state.* **economies, economize, economizes, economized, economizing, economic, economics, economical, economically, economist**

edit | **ěd'**ǐt | v. To correct errors in writing to make it ready for publication: *will edit the book.* **edits, edited, editing, editor, editors, editorial, editorially, editorialize, edition**

editor | **ěd'**ǐ tər | n. Someone who makes written work ready for publication by correcting errors, revising, etc.: *gave the editor her story.* [see *edit*]

educate | **ěj'**o̅o̅ kāt' | v. To teach; provide with knowledge: *will educate the students.* **educates, educated, educating, educator, education, educations, educational**

education | **ěj'**o̅o̅ kā'shən | n. Instruction; learning: *a college education.* [see *educate*]

effect | ǐ **fěkt'** | n. A result; an influence: *produced the desired effect.* **effects, effected, effecting, effective, effectively, effectiveness, effectual, effectually**

effective | ǐ **fěk'**tǐv | adj. Producing the result that is desired: *an effective exercise.* [see *effect*]

either | **ē'**thər | adj. One or the other: *either book.*

embarrass | ěm **băr'**əs | v. To feel self-conscious or not at ease; cause someone to feel self-conscious: *won't embarrass her by asking for a speech.* **embarrasses, embarrassed, embarrassing, embarrassingly, embarrassment**

embarrassment | ěm **băr'**əs mənt | n. The state of feeling self-conscious or not at ease: *felt embarrassment when she fell.* [see *embarrass*]

endurance | ěn **do̅o̅r'**əns | adj. Of endurance: *endurance race.* n. The ability to withstand pain, difficulty, stress, etc.: *the endurance required to climb the mountain.* [see *endure*]

endure | ěn **do̅o̅r'** | n. To continue to exist; bear up under: *will endure many hardships.* **endures, endured, enduring, enduringly, endurable, endurably, endurance**

engage | ěn **gāj'** | v. To be occupied with; take part: *to engage in an activity.* **engages, engaged, engaging, engagingly, engagement**

England | **ǐng'**glənd | n. The largest division of the United Kingdom, occupying the southern part of Great Britain: *a cousin from England.* **English**

enlargement | ěn **lärj'**mənt | n. **1.** Something that has been enlarged: *enlargement of the portrait.* **2.** The act or condition of being made larger: *enlargement of the house.* [see *large*]

enormous | ǐ **nôr'**məs | adj. Huge; very great in size or extent: *an enormous banquet.* **enormously, enormousness, enormity**

enter | ĕn′tər | *v.* To go into; come into: *will enter by the large gate.* **enters, entered, entering, entrance, entrances, entrant**

entertain | ĕn′tər tān′ | *v.* To amuse: *will entertain with a story.* **entertains, entertained, entertaining, entertainingly, entertainer, entertainment**

entertainment | ĕn′tər tān′mənt | *n.* Amusement: *a show for your entertainment.* [see *entertain*]

entrance | ĕn′trəns | *adj.* Of an entrance: *entrance ramp. n.* The place by which to enter; the door: *the entrance to the theater.* [see *enter*]

envy | ĕn′vē | *n.* A feeling of resentment or jealousy: *felt envy towards the winner.* **envies, envied, envying, envious**

equip | ĭ kwĭp′ | *v.* To provide what is needed; supply the necessities for: *will equip ourselves for the camping trip.* **equips, equipped, equipping, equipment**

equipment | ĭ kwĭp′mənt | *n.* The items that are required for a special purpose; supplies: *sports equipment.* [see *equip*]

equipped | ĭ kwĭpt′ | *v.* Provided what was needed: *equipped each scout.* [see *equip*]

escapade | ĕs′kə pād′ | *n.* A carefree adventure: *an escapade at the beach.* [see *escape*]

escape | ĭ skāp′ | *v.* To break out of confinement; become free: *to escape from the heat.* **escapes, escaped, escaping, escaper, escapee, escapade, escapades**

especially | ĭ spĕsh′ə lē | *adv.* Very; particularly: *especially generous.*

essay | ĕs′ā′ | *n.* A fairly short composition on a subject, often presenting a personal view: *wrote an essay on pollution.* **essays, essayist**

essence | ĕs′əns | *n.* The quality or qualities which make something what it is; the most important part or parts: *the essence of happiness.* **essences, essential, essentials, essentially**

estimate | ĕs′tə mĭt | *n.* A calculation; guess: *a rough estimate.* — | ĕs′tə māt | *v.* To figure or approximate; *will estimate costs.* **estimates, estimated, estimating, estimation, estimator**

evidence | ĕv′ĭ dəns | *n.* Something providing proof: *evidence of my innocence.* **evidences, evidenced, evidencing, evident, evidently**

examination | ĭg zăm′ə nā′shən | *n.* **1.** The act of observing carefully: *examination of the plant.* **2.** A test: *eye examination.* [see *examine*]

examine | ĭg zăm′ĭn | *v.* To look at closely: *will examine the sick cat.* **examines, examined, examining, examiner, examination, examinations**

examines | ĭg zăm′ĭnz | *v.* Looks at or studies carefully: *examines the plants.* [see *examine*]

exceed | ĭk sēd′ | *v.* To be greater than or more than: *won't exceed the limits.* **exceeds, exceeded, exceeding, exceedingly**

exceedingly | ĭk sē′dĭng lē | *adv.* Extremely: *exceedingly happy.* [see *exceed*]

excel | ĭk sĕl′ | *v.* To do better or to be better than others: *to excel in science.* **excels, excelled, excelling, excellent, excellently, excellence, excellency**

excellent | ĕk′sə lənt | *adj.* Extremely high in quality; superb: *an excellent dinner.* [see *excel*]

except | ĭk sĕpt′ | *prep.* Other than: *everyone except her.* **excepted, excepting, exception, exceptions, exceptional, exceptionally, exceptionable, exceptionably**

exception | ĭk sĕp′shən | *n.* A case not conforming to the accepted rules: *the exception to the rule.* [see *except*]

excess | ĕk′sĕs′ | *adj.* Beyond what is required: *excess water in the plant. n.* **1.** A surplus; extra amount: *an excess of food.* **2.** The condition of going beyond what is reasonable, normal, or proper: *an excess of snow.* **excesses, excessive, excessively, excessiveness**

excessive | ĭk sĕs′ĭv | *adj.* Greater than what is reasonable, normal, or proper: *excessive exercise.* [see *excess*]

execute | ĕk′ĭ kyōōt′ | *v.* **1.** To put into use or effect: *will execute the plans.* **2.** To carry out: *to execute the teacher's wishes.* **executes, executed, executing, executive, executives, execution, executioner, executor**

executive | ĭg zĕk′yə tĭv | *adj.* **1.** Relating to an executive, a person who manages or administrates in an organization: *an executive meeting.* **2.** Having the responsibility and power to put laws into effect: *executive decision.* [see *execute*]

ă pat / ā pay / â care / ä father / ĕ pet / ē be / ĭ pit / ī pie / î fierce / ŏ pot / ō go / ô paw, for / oi oil / ōō book /
ōō boot / ou out / ŭ cut / û fur / *th* the / th thin / hw which / zh vision / ə ago, item, pencil, atom, circus
©1977 by Houghton Mifflin Company. Reprinted by permission from THE AMERICAN HERITAGE SCHOOL DICTIONARY.

exist | ĭg **zĭst**′ | v. To live; have life: *if these flowers exist all summer.* **exists, existed, existing, existence, existences, existent**

existence | ĭg **zĭs**′tǝns | n. The fact of being; life: *a lonely existence on the island.* [see *exist*]

expect | ĭk **spekt**′ | v. To look forward to; believe will happen: *will expect a visit.* **unexpected, unexpectedly, unexpectedness**

experience | ĭk **spîr**′ē ǝns | n. Skill and knowledge gained through practice: *experience in writing.* **experiences, experienced, experiencing**

experiment | ĭk **spěr**′ǝ mǝnt | n. A test performed to demonstrate a fact, prove a theory, try out something new, etc.: *did an experiment with the chemicals.* **experiments, experimented, experimenting, experimental, experimentation, experimenter**

explode | ĭk **splōd**′ | v. 1. To burst forth suddenly and noisily: *will explode with laughter.* 2. To blow up: *should the bomb explode.* **explodes, exploded, exploding, explosion, explosive**

expose | ĭk **spōz**′ | v. 1. To leave or lay open without protection: *to expose to the cold.* 2. To cause film to react to light: *will expose the film in the lab.* **exposes, exposed, exposing, exposure, exposures, exposition**

exposure | ĭk **spō**′zhǝr | n. 1. The leaving of something unprotected: *an exposure to the sun.* 2. The processing of photographic film: *a clear exposure.* [see *expose*]

extreme | ĭk **strēm**′ | adj. Intense and severe: *an extreme reaction.* **extremes, extremely, extremity**

F

fail | fāl | v. To be unsuccessful in trying to do something: *fail to agree.* **fails, failed, failing, failingly, failer, failure, failures**

failure | **fāl**′yǝr | n. A lack of success: *failure to complete the race.* [see *fail*]

fashion | **făsh**′ǝn | n. 1. A way of dressing; style: *elegant fashion.* 2. A way of doing: *his fashion of skiing.* **fashions, fashioned, fashioning, fashionable, fashionably, fashioner**

fatal | **fāt**′l | adj. Causing death: *a fatal disease.* [see *fate*]

fate | fāt | n. A thing that happens to a person or another thing: *the fate of that plant.* **fates, fated, fatal, fateful, fatally, fatality**

fear | fîr | n. The feeling of being afraid: *a fear of snakes.* **fears, feared, fearing, fearful, fearfully, fearfulness, fearless, fearlessly, fearlessness**

fearless | **fîr**′lĭs | adj. Without fear; unafraid: *a fearless acrobat.* [see *fear*]

feature | **fē**′chǝr | n. 1. A distinct part or quality of something: *a feature of the product.* 2. Part of the face, as an eye, nose, mouth, etc.: *an attractive feature.* **features, featured, featuring**

federal | **fěd**′ǝr ǝl | adj. Relating to a type of government in which individual states keep some powers while united under a central authority: *federal law.* [see *federate*]

federate | **fěd**′ǝ rāt′ | v. To form into a union or a federal: *will federate the states.* **federates, federated, federating, federal, federally, federation, federations, federalist**

feeble | **fē**′bǝl | adj. Weak; very frail: *a feeble voice.* **feebler, feeblest, feebly, feebleness**

fiber | **fī**′bǝr | n. A thread; a material made of threadlike parts: *a natural fiber for weaving.* **fibers, fibered, fibrous**

fierce | fîrs | adj. Violent; very strong: *a fierce storm.* **fiercer, fiercest, fiercely, fierceness**

fiery | **fīr**′ē | adj. Burning; flaming: *a fiery light.* [see *fire*]

fire | fîr | n. A blaze; flame, light, and heat caused by something that is burning: *warming our hands by the fire.* **fires, fired, firing, fiery, fieriness**

forfeit | **fôr**′fĭt | v. To give up something as a kind of penalty: *will forfeit the prize.* **forfeits, forfeited, forfeiting, forfeitable, forfeiter**

formal | **fôr**′mǝl | adj. Relating to something done officially, according to accepted rules: *made a formal request for aid.* **formals, formally, formality, formalize**

former | **fôr**′mǝr | adj. Earlier than the one or ones specified: *the former leader.* **formerly**

formerly | **fôr**′mǝr lē | adv. At a previous time; once: *formerly employed.* [see *former*]

fortunate | **fôr**′chǝ nĭt | adj. Lucky: *a fortunate discovery.* [see *fortune*]

fortune | **fôr**′chǝn | n. Chance; good or bad luck: *had good fortune.* **fortunes, fortunate, fortunately, unfortunate, unfortunately**

fracture | **frăk**′chǝr | n. 1. A breaking of a bone: *a fracture in his arm.* 2. A crack: *a fracture in the rock.* **fractures, fractured, fracturing**

fragrance | **frā′**grəns | *n.* A pleasing odor: *fragrance of perfume.* **fragrant, fragrantly**

fragrant | **frā′**grənt | *adj.* Having a pleasing odor: *fragrant roses.* [see *fragrance*]

frail | frāl | *adj.* Weak or fragile: *frail after the illness.* **frailer, frailest, frailly, frailness, frailty**

furious | **fyoŏr′**ē əs | *adj.* Extremely angry; enraged: *furious about the broken vase.* [see *fury*]

fury | **fyoŏr′**ē | *n.* Extreme and violent anger: *felt fury after the argument.* **furor, furious, furiously**

G

gallery | **găl′**ə rē | *n.* A special room or building for displaying collections of art: *visited the gallery on a class trip.* **galleries**

general | **jĕn′**ər əl | *adj.* Common to most; widespread: *a general interest.* **generals, generalize, generalizes, generalized, generalizing, generalist, generality, generalities, generalization, generally**

generally | **jĕn′**ər ə lē | *adv.* Usually; in most cases: *generally active.* [see *general*]

generate | **jĕn′**ə rāt′ | *v.* **1.** To produce; bring about by a physical or chemical process: *can generate light.* **2.** To create: *will generate a solution.* **3.** To produce offspring: *will generate five puppies.* **generates, generated, generating, generation, generations, generator**

generation | **jĕn′**ə rā′shən | *n.* All offspring in the same stage of descent from a common parent or parents: *second generation of cousins.* [see *generate*]

generosity | **jĕn′**ər rŏs′ĭ tē | *n.* Willingness to share: *showed caring and generosity.* **generous, generously, generousness**

generous | **jĕn′**ər əs | *adj.* Unselfish: *a generous person.* [see *generosity*]

geography | jē ŏg′rə fē | *n.* The physical features of a particular location: *studied the geography of Colorado.* **geographies, geographic, geographical, geographer**

germ | jûrm | *n.* A small organic structure or cell from which a new organism may develop: *a disease-causing germ.* **germs, germy**

germs | jûrmz | *n.* Microorganisms that can cause disease: *germs in the air.* [see *germ*]

giant | jī′ənt | *adj.* Huge: *a giant hole.* *n.* A person or creature of immense size: *the giant in the story.* **giants, giantness, gigantic, gigantically**

gigantic | jī găn′tĭk | *adj.* Extremely large, powerful, etc.: *gigantic gorilla.* [see *giant*]

glimpse | glĭmps | *n.* A quick, quite short view: *glimpse from the train window.* **glimpses, glimpsed, glimpsing**

glorious | glôr′ē əs | *adj.* Magnificent; very beautiful or splendid: *glorious weather.* [see *glory*]

glory | glôr′ē | *n.* A period of splendor; great beauty: *the glory of the sunset.* **glories, gloried, glorying, glorify, glorious, gloriously, gloriousness, glorification**

gopher | gō′fər | *adj.* Of a gopher: *gopher teeth.* *n.* A small burrowing animal with pouches in the cheek: *gopher sitting near its hole.* **gophers**

gorgeous | gôr′jəs | *adj.* Very beautiful: *a gorgeous necklace.* **gorgeously, gorgeousness**

govern | gŭv′ərn | *v.* To rule or control: *will govern the island.* **governs, governed, governing, governors, governess, government**

governor | gŭv′ər nər | *n.* A person elected as an official of a state, province, colony, city, etc.: *became governor of the state.* [see *govern*]

grace | grās | *n.* A charming or appealing characteristic: *talked with grace and wit.* **graces, graced, gracing, graceful, gracious, graciousness**

gracious | grā′shəs | *adj.* Courteous; showing grace and charm: *a gracious host.* [see *grace*]

grade | grād | *n.* One step in a series of steps, stages, ranks, etc.: *in the seventh grade.* **grades, graded, grading, grader, gradual, gradually, graduate, graduates, graduated, graduating, gradualness, graduation**

gradually | grăj′oō ə lē | *adv.* Little by little; slowly: *gradually finished.* [see *grade*]

graduate | grăj′oō ĭt | *n.* A person who has received an academic degree: *a high-school graduate.* [see *grade*]

ă pat / ā pay / â care / ä father / ĕ pet / ē be / ĭ pit / ī pie / î fierce / ŏ pot / ō go / ô paw, for / oi oil / oŏ book / oō boot / ou out / ŭ cut / û fur / *th* the / th thin / hw which / zh vision / ə ago, item, pencil, atom, circus
©1977 by Houghton Mifflin Company. Reprinted by permission from THE AMERICAN HERITAGE SCHOOL DICTIONARY.

grammar | **grăm'**ər | *n.* The rules of a language that explain how sentences are put together: *will study English grammar.* **grammarian, grammatical, grammatically**

grease | grēs | *n.* A thick, oily substance such as animal fat: *spilled grease on the stove.* **greases, greased, greasing, greasy, greasier, greasiest, greasiness**

grieve | grēv | *v.* To feel very sad; be filled with grief: *to grieve the death of their pet.* **grieves, grieved, grieving, grievingly, grievous, grieviously, grievance, griever, grief**

grim | grĭm | *adj.* Stern in action or appearance; somber or gloomy: *a grim outlook on life.* **grimmer, grimmest, grimly**

groove | grōōv | *n.* **1.** The narrow track on a phonograph record in which the needle moves: *when the needle misses the groove.* **2.** A track or furrow: *a groove on the side of the road.* **grooves, grooved, grooving, groovy**

guard | gärd | *n.* A person who guards, protects or carefully watches someone or something: *a guard at the prison.* **guards, guarded, guarding, guardedly, guardingly, guardian, guardians, guardianship**

guardian | **gär'**dē ən | *n.* **1.** A person legally responsible for someone or something: *guardian of the child.* **2.** A person who guards or protects someone or something: *guardian of the president.* [see *guard*]

guidance | **gīd'**ns | *n.* Direction; leadership: *provided guidance for me.* [see *guide*]

guide | gīd | *v.* To lead or direct: *will guide the campers along the trail.* **guides, guided, guiding, guider, guidance**

H

harried | **hăr'**ēd | *adj.* Worried; tormented: *the harried worker.* [see *harry*]

harry | **hăr'**ē | *v.* To harass; disturb constantly: *to harry the supervisor with questions.* **harries, harried, harrying**

haunt | hônt | *v.* To visit in the form of a ghost: *to haunt the attic.* **haunts, haunted, haunting, hauntingly, haunter**

hedge | hĕj | *n.* A boundary formed by a dense row of low shrubs or trees: *a hedge dividing the properties.* **hedges**

helicopter | **hĕl'**ĭ kŏp'tər | *n.* A type of aircraft supported by rotors or propellers rather than wings: *rode in the helicopter.* **helicopters**

hindsight | **hīnd'**sīt' | *n.* The ability to see what should have been done, after something is over: *used hindsight rather than foresight.*

hinge | hĭnj | *n.* A device with joints on which a door, gate, cover, etc., swings: *the hinge on the door.* **hinges, hinged, hinging**

historical | hĭ **stôr'**ĭ kəl | *adj.* Relating to history, the study of past events: *historical novel.* [see *history*]

history | **hĭs'**tə rē | *n.* The events of the past that led to the present: *studied the history of the war.* **histories, historian, historic, historical, historically**

hitch | hĭch | *v.* To fasten by using a hook, ring, rope, etc.: *will hitch the ox to the plow.* **hitches, hitched, hitching**

hitched | hĭcht | *v.* Fastened or hooked to: *hitched to the wagon.* [see *hitch*]

hobbies | **hŏb'**ēz | *n.* Favorite pastimes: *the hobbies of painting and singing.* [see *hobby*]

hobby | **hŏb'**ē | *n.* A favorite pastime: *collected stamps for a hobby.* **hobbies, hobbyist**

honor | **ŏn'**ər | *n.* Great respect or high regard: *showed honor to the president.* **honors, honored, honoring, honorable, honorably, honorary**

honorable | **ŏn'**ər ə bəl | *adj.* Showing a strong sense of what is right or proper: *honorable behavior.* [see *honor*]

horrid | **hôr'**ĭd | *adj.* Very disagreeable, unpleasant, etc.: *having horrid weather.* [see *horror*]

horrifying | **hôr'**ə fī'ĭng | *adj.* Terrifying: *horrifying news.* [see *horror*]

horror | **hôr'**ər | *adj.* Relating to something that creates terror or fear: *horror story.* *n.* Great terror or fear: *felt horror after the accident.* **horrors, horrible, horribly, horribleness, horrify, horrifies, horrified, horrifying, horrifyingly, horrid, horridly, horridness**

human | **hyōō'**mən | *adj.* Of persons: *human understanding.* **humans, humane, humanely, humanize, humaneness, humanity**

humane | hyōō **mān'** | *adj.* Kind; full of mercy: *humane act.* [see *human*]

hygiene | **hī'**jēn' | *n.* Methods and science for promoting good health and preventing disease: *studied hygiene in school.* **hygienic, hygienically, hygienist**

I

ice | īs | *n.* Frozen water: *cold enough for ice.* **ices, iced, icing, icy, icicle, icicles**

icicle | ī′sĭ kəl | *n.* A pointed stick of hanging ice: *icicle on the branch.* [see *ice*]

image | ĭm′ĭj | *n.* A mental picture of something: *an image in my mind.* **images, imagine, imagines, imagined, imagining, imagination, imaginations, imaginative, imaginary, imagery**

imagination | ĭ măj′ə nā′shən | *n.* The ability to form pictures in the mind: *a lively imagination.* [see *image*]

imagine | ĭ măj′ĭn | *v.* To form a picture in the mind: *can imagine a distant place.* [see *image*]

immense | ĭ měns′ | *adj.* Of very great size or extent; huge: *immense canyon.* **immensely, immensity, immenseness**

impress | ĭm prĕs ′ | *v.* To fix firmly in the mind, especially by force or strong influence: *will impress our needs upon them.* **impresses, impressed, impressing, impression, impressions, impressionable, impressive, impressively, impressionism, impressionist**

impression | ĭm prĕsh′ən | *n.* A vague but lasting idea or feeling about someone or something: *a good impression.* [see *impress*]

improvise | ĭm′prə vīz′ | *v.* **1.** To create or compose without preparation: *will improvise a speech.* **2.** To make do: *can improvise a meal.* **improvises, improvised, improvising, improviser, improvisation**

incident | ĭn′sĭ dənt | *n.* An occurrence or event, often a minor one: *incident on the tennis court.* **incidents, incidental, incidentally, incidence**

indicate | ĭn′dĭ kāt′ | *v.* **1.** To make known; show: *indicate the degree of pain.* **2.** To point out; identify: *indicate the color.* **indicates, indicated, indicating, indicator, indication**

indifferent | ĭn dĭf′rənt | *adj.* Showing no interest; uninvolved: *an indifferent attitude.* [see *differ*]

individual | ĭn′də vĭj′o͞o əl | *adj.* For or by one person: *individual amounts.* **individuals, individually, individualist, individuality, individualize**

industrial | ĭn dŭs′trē əl | *adj.* Relating to industry, the manufacture and production of something: *an industrial worker.* [see *industry*]

industry | ĭn′də strē | *n.* A branch of business, trade, or manufacturing: *motion-picture industry.* **industries, industrial, industrious, industriously, industrialize, industrialism**

influence | ĭn′flo͞o əns | *n.* The power to create effects or changes: *my influence on them.* *v.* To have an effect on: *influence my thoughts.* **influences, influenced, influencing, influential**

inhabit | ĭn hăb′ĭt | *v.* To live in: *will inhabit this house.* **inhabits, inhabited, inhabiting, inhabitant, inhabitants**

inhabitant | ĭn hăb′ĭ tənt | *n.* A resident: *an inhabitant of the building.* [see *inhabit*]

initial | ĭ nĭsh′əl | *n.* **1.** The beginning letter of a name or a word: *initial of his last name.* *adj.* First: *initial speech of the meeting.* **initials, initialed, initialing, initially, initiate, initiative**

innocent | ĭn′ə sənt | *adj.* **1.** Not guilty of a crime or fault of which one has been accused: *innocent of the robbery.* **2.** Very naive; not sophisticated: *an innocent child.* **innocently, innocence**

instance | ĭn′stəns | *n.* An illustration, case, or example: *one instance of progress.* **instant, instants, instantly, instantaneous**

instrument | ĭn′strə mənt | *n.* A device used to make music: *a musical instrument.* **instruments, instrumental, instrumentally, instrumentalist**

insult | ĭn sŭlt′ | *v.* To speak to in a contemptuous way: *should not insult the teacher.* **insults, insulted, insulting**

insulted | ĭn sŭl′tĭd | *v.* Spoke to in an offensive manner: *insulted the visitors.* [see *insult*]

intellect | ĭn′tl ĕkt′ | *n.* The capacity to think, reason, and learn: *great intellect for mathematics.* **intellects, intellectual, intellectually, intellectualist, intellectualize, intelligent, intelligently, intelligence**

intelligent | ĭn tĕl′ə jənt | *adj.* Very wise and thoughtful: *intelligent decision.* [see *intellect*]

interfere | ĭn′tər fîr′ | *v.* To act as an obstacle; conflict: *won't interfere with my plans.* **interferes, interfered, interfering, interference**

ă pat / ā pay / â care / ä father / ĕ pet / ē be / ĭ pit / ī pie / î fierce / ŏ pot / ō go / ô paw, for / oi oil / o͝o book / o͞o boot / ou out / ŭ cut / û fur / th the / th thin / hw which / zh vision / ə ago, item, pencil, atom, circus
©1977 by Houghton Mifflin Company. Reprinted by permission from THE AMERICAN HERITAGE SCHOOL DICTIONARY.

interior | ĭn tîr'ē ər | *adj.* Relating to the inside of something, such as a building: *interior design.* *n.* The inside of something, such as a building: *the interior of the school.* **interiors**

international | ĭn'tər nǎsh'ən əl | *adj.* Relating to two or more nations or nationalities: *an international conference.* **internationally**

interrupt | ĭn'tə rǔpt' | *v.* To break in on: *won't interrupt the discussion.* **interrupts, interrupted, interrupting, interruption, interruptive, interrupter**

interval | ĭn'tər vəl | *n.* A period of time in between: *an interval of six months.* **intervals**

interview | ĭn'tər vyōō' | *n.* A face-to-face meeting between people: *interview with the manager.* **interviews, interviewed, interviewing, interviewer, interviewee**

invest | ĭn vĕst' | *v.* **1.** To use or spend for a future benefit: *will invest energy in building the clubhouse.* **2.** To put money into something in order to gain a profit, earn interest, etc.: *should invest in my business.* **invests, invested, investing, investor, investment**

investigate | ĭn vĕs'tĭ gāt' | *v.* To search; look thoroughly into: *will investigate the mysterious noise.* **investigates, investigated, investigating, investigator, investigation**

invisible | ĭn vĭz'ə bəl | *adj.* Not able to be seen: *an invisible gas.* [see *visible*]

irony | ī'rə nē | *n.* **1.** Sarcasm: *an insult full of irony.* **2.** An event or outcome that is opposite of what would be expected: *irony of his mistake.* **ironies, ironic, ironical, ironically**

irrigate | ĭr'ĭ gāt' | *v.* To supply land with water, using a system of ditches, sprinklers, etc.: *will irrigate the fields.* **irrigates, irrigated, irrigating, irrigation, irrigator**

J

jar | jär | *v.* To shock; disturb: *might jar me with the noise.* **jars, jarred, jarring**

jarring | jär'ĭng | *adj.* Irritating or disturbing: *jarring music.* [see *jar*]

journal | jûr'nəl | *n.* A record of daily events, transactions, etc.: *wrote in my journal.* **journals, journalism, journalist**

joy | joi | *n.* A feeling of much happiness: *the joy of giving.* **joyful, joyous, joyless, joyously**

joyous | joi'əs | *adj.* Feeling or causing happiness: *a joyous event.* [see *joy*]

juice | jōōs | *n.* The liquid in plant tissue: *juice of an orange.* **juices, juiced, juicing, juicy, juicier, juiciest**

juiciest | jōō'sē ĭst | *adj.* Filled with the most juice or liquid: *the juiciest plums.* [see *juice*]

just | jŭst | *adj.* Fair; showing honest impartiality: *a just decision.* **justly, justness, justice, justify, justified, justifying, justifier, justification**

justice | jŭs'tĭs | *n.* Fair treatment: *received justice.* [see *just*]

K

kindle | kĭn'dl | *v.* To light; set on fire: *will kindle a camp fire.* **kindles, kindled, kindling**

kindling | kĭnd'lĭng | *n.* Very small pieces of wood used for starting a fire: *gathered twigs for kindling.* [see *kindle*]

knight | nīt | *n.* A man raised to an honorable rank, usually serving a king or feudal lord during the Middle Ages: *a knight of the king's court.* **knights, knighted, knighting, knightly**

L

laboratory | lăb'rə tôr'ē | *n.* A place, such as a room or building, equipped for research: *tested the substance in the laboratory.* **laboratories**

large | lärj | *adj.* Bigger than average in size or amount: *a large package.* **enlarge, enlarges, enlarged, enlarging, enlarger, enlargement, enlargements**

late | lāt | *adj.* Not on time; tardy: *a late visitor.* **latter, latterly**

latter | lăt'ər | *n.* The second of two; the last: *chose the latter of the plans.* *adj.* Being the second of two: *at the latter date.* [see *late*]

legal | lē'gəl | *adj.* Relating to the administration, procedures, and profession of the law: *legal document.* **legally, legality, legalize, legalizes, legalized, legalizing, legalization**

legislate | lĕj'ĭs lāt' | *v.* To pass or to make laws: *legislate a proposal about pollution.* **legislates, legislated, legislating, legislator, legislature, legislatures, legislation, legislative**

legislature | lĕg'ĭs lā'chər | *n.* A group of persons with power to make laws: *a meeting of the legislature.* [see *legislate*]

leisure | lē'zhər | *adj.* Free; relating to free time: *leisure hours after school.* *n.* Free time: *enjoyed several hours of leisure.* **leisurely, leisureliness**

levee | lĕv′ē | *n.* A mass of earth, concrete, etc., put up along a river to prevent flooding: *the storm cracked the levee.* **levees, leveed, leveeing**

levy | lĕv′ē | *v.* To place or collect some kind of fee: *to levy a fine.* **levies, levied, levying**

liberate | lĭb′ə rāt′ | *v.* To set free: *will liberate the bird.* **liberates, liberated, liberating, liberation, liberty, liberties, liberal, liberator**

library | lī′brĕr′ē | *n.* A room or building with a collection of books, magazines, films, records, etc.: *a tape from the library.* **libraries, librarian**

license | lī′səns | *n.* A piece of paper, a card, or a metal plate showing permission given by law to do something: *will need a license.* **licenses, licensed, licensing, licenser**

lieutenant | lōō tĕn′ənt | *n.* An officer in one of the armed services: *by order of the lieutenant.* **lieutenants**

like | līk | *v.* To regard with favor; have friendly feelings toward: *to like animals.* **likes, liked, liking, liken, likely, likelier, likeliest, likeliness, likeness**

likeliest | līk′lē ĭst | *adj.* Most apt or probable: *likeliest candidate for treasurer.* [see *like*]

limit | lĭm′ĭt | *n.* A point beyond which a person cannot go: *reached the limit of the land.* **limits, limited, limitless, limitation, limitations**

limitation | lĭm′ĭ tā′shən | *n.* A restriction; something that limits or restricts: *a limitation on the number of passengers.* [see *limit*]

linger | lĭng′gər | *v.* To stay in a place longer, as if not willing to leave: *will linger at the beach.* **lingers, lingered, lingering, lingerer**

literacy | lĭt′ər ə sē | *adj.* Relating to the ability to read and write: *a literacy test.* [see *literate*]

literate | lĭt′ər ĭt | *adj.* Capable of reading and writing: *the literate student.* **literacy, literately, literateness, literature, literatures, literary**

literature | lĭt′ər ə chər | *n.* A collection of writing in prose or verse: *studied French literature.* [see *literate*]

local | lō′kəl | *adj.* Relating to a limited area: *only a local storm.* **locally, locality, localize, localization, locale**

locally | lō′kə lē | *adv.* Nearby: *lived locally.* [see *local*]

lone | lōn | *adj.* Single; without others: *a lone wolf in the forest.* **lonely, lonelier, loneliest, lonesome, loner, loneliness**

loneliness | lōn′lē nĭs | *n.* Sadness caused from being alone: *loneliness when friends are away.* [see *lone*]

love | lŭv | *n.* A feeling of deep affection: *love for my sister.* **loves, loved, loving, lovable, lovely, lovelier, loveliest, loveliness**

loveliness | lŭv′lē nĭs | *n.* Beauty: *the loveliness of the forest.* [see *love*]

lunch | lŭnch | *n.* A meal that is eaten around noon: *had lunch in the cafeteria.* **lunches, lunched, lunching, luncheon, luncheons**

luncheon | lŭn′chən | *n.* A meal, often formal, that is eaten around midday: *our club's annual luncheon.* [see *lunch*]

luxury | lŭg′zhə rē | *n.* **1.** Something that is not considered essential but is an extravagance: *because the diamond was a luxury.* **2.** A fancy environment: *to travel in luxury.* **luxuries, luxurious, luxuriously, luxuriant**

M

magnificence | măg nĭf′ĭ səns | *n.* Greatness; splendidness: *the mountain's magnificence.* **magnificent, magnificently**

magnificent | măg nĭf′ĭ sənt | *adj.* Very grand: *a magnificent painting.* [see *magnificence*]

major | mā′jər | *adj.* Large, important, or leading: *the major reason for failure.* **majors, majority, majorities**

majorities | mə jôr′ĭ tēz | *n.* The larger numbers or parts: *majorities of several sections.* [see *major*]

mammal | măm′əl | *n.* Any of a group of warm-blooded vertebrate animals such as dogs, cats, whales, bats, and human beings: *will study the behavior of this mammal.* **mammals**

manage | măn′ĭj | *v.* To direct; supervise: *will manage a business.* **managers, managed, managing, manager, managers, management**

manager | măn′ĭ jər | *n.* A person who supervises: *a store manager.* [see *manage*]

mansion | măn′shən | *n.* A large house: *lived in a mansion.* **mansions**

ă pat / ā pay / â care / ä father / ĕ pet / ē be / ĭ pit / ī pie / î fierce / ŏ pot / ō go / ô paw, for / oi oil / ŏŏ book / ōō boot / ou out / ŭ cut / û fur / *th* the / th thin / hw which / zh vision / ə ago, item, pencil, atom, circus
©1977 by Houghton Mifflin Company. Reprinted by permission from THE AMERICAN HERITAGE SCHOOL DICTIONARY.

margin | **mär′**jĭn | *n.* The extra amount of something, beyond what is necessary: *had a margin of only two.* **margins, margined, margining, marginal, marginally**

marginal | **mär′**jə nəl | *adj.* Barely acceptable: *a marginal grade on the test.* [see *margin*]

marvel | **mär′**vəl | *v.* To feel surprised, astonished, or filled with wonder: *will marvel at the unusual statue.* **marvels, marveled, marveling, marvelous, marvelously**

marvelous | **mär′**və ləs | *adj.* Wonderful; creating a feeling of surprise: *a marvelous view of the city.* [see *marvel*]

mathematics | măth′ə **măt′**ĭks | *n.* The study of numbers and forms: *a degree in mathematics.* **mathematical, mathematically, mathematician, math**

mean | mēn | *adj.* Cruel; unkind: *a mean comment.* **meaner, meanest, meanly, meanness**

meanness | **mēn′**nĭs | *n.* Cruelty or unkindness: *meanness of the spoiled child.* [see *mean*]

mechanic | mə **kăn′**ĭk | *n.* A person who works with machines or tools: *took the car to a mechanic.* **mechanics, mechanism, mechanize, mechanical, mechanically**

mechanical | mə **kăn′**ĭ kəl | *adv.* Relating to machines or tools; operated by a machine: *a mechanical error.* [see *mechanic*]

medal | **mĕd′**l | *n.* A piece of metal, usually coin-shaped, given as an award: *won the medal for first place.* **medals, medallion, medalist**

melt | mĕlt | *v.* To change from a solid to a liquid state by applying heat: *will melt the ice.* **melts, melted, melting, molten**

memorable | **mĕm′**ər ə bəl | *adj.* Remarkable; unforgettable: *a memorable concert.* [see *memory*]

memorial | mə **môr′**ē əl | *adj.* Honoring the memory of a special event or person: *a memorial statue.* [see *memory*]

memories | **mĕm′**ə rēz | *n.* Events remembered from the past: *memories of childhood.* [see *memory*]

memory | **mĕm′**ə rē | *n.* **1.** An event remembered from the past: *a memory of happier times.* **2.** The ability to store past experiences in the mind and to recall them: *a memory for dates.* **3.** Honor or respect for a person, thing, or event in the past: *memory for those who died in battle.* **memories, memorize, memorizes, memorized, memorizing, memorization, memorizer, memorable, memorably, memorial, memorials, memorialize, memorabilia, memorandum, memo, memoir**

mere | mîr | *adj.* Simple; being nothing more than what is stated or specified: *mere words without action.* **merely, merest**

might | mīt | *n.* **1.** Great force and power: *the might of the tidal wave.* **2.** Bravery: *the might of the soldier.* **mighty, mightier, mightiest, mightily, mightiness**

mightiest | **mī′**tē ĭst | *adj.* Strongest and bravest: *the mightiest king.* [see *might*]

minor | **mī′**nər | *adj.* Smaller in size or amount: *a minor inconvenience.* **minority, minorities**

minorities | mĭ **nôr′**ĭ tēz | *n.* The smaller numbers or parts; groups of people different in some way from the majority: *problems of the minorities.* [see *minor*]

mischief | **mĭs′**chĭf | *n.* Behavior that causes trouble, often not on purpose: *caused mischief at the party.* **mischievous, mischievously**

miserable | **mĭz′**ər ə bəl | *adj.* **1.** Very bad; awful: *a miserable cold.* **2.** Very unhappy: *in a miserable mood.* [see *misery*]

misery | **mĭz′**ə rē | *n.* Distress or suffering, usually lasting for a time: *was in misery due to the pain in her leg.* **miseries, miserable, miserably, miserableness**

misspell | mĭs **spĕl′** | *v.* To spell a word incorrectly: *will misspell two words.* [see *spell*]

misuse | mĭs **yōō z′** | *v.* To use in the wrong way; use incorrectly: *might misuse the word.* [see *use*]

moist | moist | *adj.* Somewhat wet; damp: *a moist cloth.* **moisten, moistens, moistened, moistening, moisture, moistness, moisturize, moisturizes, moisturized, moisturizing**

moisten | **moi′**sən | *v.* To make somewhat damp: *will moisten the stamp.* [see *moist*]

moisture | **mois′**chər | *n.* A small amount of condensed liquid: *a dew-like moisture.* [see *moist*]

molten | **mōl′**tən | *adj.* Made liquid by applying heat: *molten silver in the mold.* [see *melt*]

monster | **mŏn′**stər | *n.* A huge creature or thing: *the imaginary monster.* **monsters, monstrous, monstrously, monstrosity**

monstrous | **mŏn′**strəs | *adj.* Extremely large in size: *monstrous mountains.* [see *monster*]

monument | **mŏn′**yə mənt | *n.* A building, statue, pillar, etc., set up to honor someone or something: *monument in the park.* **monuments, monumental, monumentally**

mosquito | mə **skē′**tō | *n.* One of a group of small, winged insects with females that bite humans and animals: *an annoying mosquito.* **mosquitoes**

mosquitoes | mə **skē′**tōz | *n.* More than one mosquito: *woods full of mosquitoes.* [see *mosquito*]

motto | **mŏt′**ō | *n.* A slogan or saying: *a motto for our team.* **mottos**

museum | myo͞o **zē′**əm | *n.* A building in which artistic, historical, scientific, or social exhibits are displayed: *the science museum.* **museums**

mustard | **mŭs′**tərd | *n.* A spicy yellowish paste made from seeds of a mustard plant: *mustard on the sandwich.* **mustards**

mysterious | mĭ **stîr′**ē əs | *adj.* Relating to a mystery; difficult to explain: *mysterious shadow on the wall.* [see *mystery*]

mystery | **mĭs′**tə rē | *n.* Anything that causes curiosity, as it is difficult to explain: *the mystery of the missing boat.* **mysteries, mysterious, mysteriously**

N

necessary | **nĕs′**ĭ sĕr′ē | *adj.* Needed: *necessary equipment.* **unnecessary, unnecessarily**

neglect | nĭ **glĕkt′** | *v.* To pay no attention to; give too little care to: *won't neglect the weedy garden.* **neglects, neglected, neglecting, negligence, negligent, negligible**

negligence | **nĕg′**lĭ jəns | *n.* The lack of proper attention to; carelessness: *if negligence caused the error.* [see *neglect*]

nerve | nûrv | *n.* A fiber in the body, extending from the central nervous system to another part of the body, that carries sense messages: *hit a nerve in my finger.* **nerves, nervous, nervously, nervousness**

nervous | **nûr′**vəs | *adj.* Anxious; quite uneasy: *nervous voice.* [see *nerve*]

nonsense | **nŏn′**sĕns′ | *n.* Foolishness; something not sensible: *because the joke was nonsense.* **nonsensical, nonsensically**

noodle | **no͞od′**l | *n.* A narrow strip of dried egg dough: *a cooked noodle.* *adj.* Made of noodles: *noodle pudding.* **noodles**

notation | nō **tā′**shən | *n.* The use of accepted symbols to represent something else in a brief, clear way: *used musical notation to record the tune.* [see *note*]

note | nōt | *n.* A written sign in music to represent a sound: *a high note.* **notes, noted, noting, notable, notate, notates, notated, notating, notation, notations**

notifies | **nō′**tə fīz′ | *v.* Informs; lets someone know: *notifies the new members.* [see *notify*]

notify | **nō′**tə fī′ | *v.* To inform: *will notify the parents.* **notifies, notified, notifying**

nuisance | **no͞o′**səns | *n.* An inconvenience or annoyance: *the nuisance of carrying the heavy package.* **nuisances**

numb | nŭm | *adj.* Without feeling or sensation: *fingers numb with cold.* **numbs, numbed, numbing, numbness**

number | **nŭm′**bər | *n.* A word that tells exactly how many: *the number for 2 plus 2.* **numbers, numbered, numbering, numeral, numerals, numerous, numerical, numerate, numerates, numerated, numerating, numeration, numerator, numeric, numerical**

numeral | **no͞o′**mər əl | *n.* A symbol used to represent a number: *an odd numeral.* [see *number*]

numerous | **no͞o′**mər əs | *adj.* Many: *numerous stars.* [see *number*]

O

occasion | ə **kā′**zhən | *n.* An event; a meaningful happening: *a memorable occasion.* **occasions, occasioned, occasioning, occasional, occasionally**

occupation | ŏk′yə **pā′**shən | *n.* A profession or a job: *the occupation of teaching.* [see *occupy*]

occupy | **ŏk′**yə pī′ | *v.* **1.** To take up; fill: *will occupy these seats.* **2.** To employ; busy oneself: *will occupy my free time with books.* **occupies, occupied, occupying, occupant, occupation, occupations, occupational**

offend | ə **fĕnd′** | *v.* To cause anger or resentment; insult: *don't offend me.* **offends, offended, offending, offender, offense, offenses, offensive, offensively, offensiveness**

ă pat / ā pay / â care / ä father / ĕ pet / ē be / ĭ pit / ī pie / î fierce / ŏ pot / ō go / ô paw, for / oi oil / o͞o book /
o͞o boot / ou out / ŭ cut / û fur / *th* the / th thin / hw which / zh vision / ə ago, item, pencil, atom, circus
©1977 by Houghton Mifflin Company. Reprinted by permission from THE AMERICAN HERITAGE SCHOOL DICTIONARY.

offense | ə **fĕns**′ | *n.* An act that causes anger or resentment: *because the offense was not on purpose.* [see *offend*]

office | ô′fĭs | *n.* **1.** A place in which work is done: *went to the doctor's office.* **2.** A position, especially in public service: *office of President.* **offices, officer, official, officially, officiate**

official | ə **fĭsh**′əl | *adj.* Of an office of authority: *official rule. n.* A person who has a position of authority: *spoke to the official.* [see *office*]

omission | ō **mĭsh**′ən | *n.* The act of leaving out someone or something: *omission of some important facts.* [see *omit*]

omit | ō **mĭt**′ | *v.* To leave out: *will omit my name from the list.* **omits, omitted, omitting, omission, omissions**

opinion | ō **pĭn**′yən | *n.* Something believed that isn't necessarily true: *my opinion about the design.* **opinions, opinionated**

oppose | ə **pōz**′ | *v.* To resist or dispute: *will oppose the unfair law.* **opposes, opposed, opposing, opposite, opposition**

orbit | **ôr**′bĭt | *n.* The path of one body around another body in space: *the orbit of the moon.* **orbits, orbited, orbiting, orbital, orbiter**

ordinary | **ôr**′dn ĕr′ē | *adj.* Customary; usual: *ordinary habits.* **ordinarily, ordinariness**

organ | **ôr**′gən | *n.* A part of a living thing that functions in a particular way: *a digestive organ.* **organs, organic, organism, organisms**

organism | **ôr**′gə nĭz′ əm | *n.* A living thing, such as a plant or animal: *studied the organism.* [see *organ*]

organization | ôr′gə nĭ **zā**′shən | *n.* **1.** The act of putting into order: *organization of my thoughts.* **2.** People or groups united together for a purpose: *join a local organization.* [see *organize*]

organize | **ôr**′gə nīz′ | *v.* **1.** To arrange in an orderly way: *will organize the work area.* **2.** To join or unite together for a purpose: *must organize the volunteers.* **organizes, organized, organizing, organization, organizations**

origin | **ôr**′ə jĭn | *n.* The source; the beginning: *the origin of life.* **origins, original, originals, originally, originality, originate, originator**

original | ə **rĭj**′ə nəl | *adj.* Not copied or imitated; new: *an original story.* [see *origin*]

ought | ôt | *v.* A word used to indicate duty or what is expected: *ought to ask first.*

oyster | **oi**′stər | *n.* A sea animal with a soft body inside of a hinged shell: *ate the oyster.* **oysters**

P

pageant | **păj**′ənt | *n.* **1.** An elaborate show or display: *a glamorous pageant.* **2.** A procession or special play: *will participate in the pageant.* **pageants, pageantry**

parallel | **păr**′ə lĕl′ | *adj.* Lying next to one another, at all points the same distance apart: *parallel strips of wood.* **parallels, paralleled**

parcel | **pär**′səl | *n.* A package: *delivered the parcel.* **parcels, parceled, parceling**

particular | pər **tĭk**′yə lər | *adj.* Specific: *a particular week.* **particulars, particularly, particularity**

particularly | pər **tĭk**′yə lər lē | *adv.* To a very great degree; especially: *particularly helpful to me.* [see *particular*]

patience | **pā**′shəns | *n.* Calm willingness to put up with a difficult situation: *has patience with the tired child.* **patient, patients, patiently**

patient | **pā**′shənt | *n.* Someone under medical care: *a patient in the hospital.* [see *patience*]

peculiar | pĭ **kyōōl**′yər | *adj.* Very unusual or strange: *a peculiar expression.* **peculiarly, peculiarity**

percent | pər **sĕnt**′ | *n.* Out of each hundred: *if only 50 percent voted.* **percents, percentage, percentages**

percentage | pər **sĕn**′tĭj | *n.* Portion or part of a whole: *a small percentage.* [see *percent*]

perfect | **pûr**′fĭkt | *adj.* Without flaws or defects: *a perfect design.* **perfects, perfected, perfecting, perfectly, perfectness, perfection, perfectionist**

perfectly | **pûr**′fĭkt lē | *adv.* Flawlessly; without errors: *perfectly painted.* [see *perfect*]

persuade | pər **swād**′ | *v.* To convince; make someone believe or do something: *will persuade us to visit.* **persuades, persuaded, persuading, persuasion, persuasive, persuasively, persuasiveness, persuader**

persuasive | pər **swā**′sĭv | *adj.* Convincing; having the power to cause someone to do something: *a persuasive reason.* [see *persuade*]

phrase | frāz | *n.* A group of words not having both a subject and a predicate: *wrote only a phrase.* **phrases, phrased, phrasing**

physical | **fĭz**′ĭ kəl | *adj.* Pertaining to the body rather than the mind: *physical exercise.* [see *physics*]

physics | **fĭz′ĭks** | *n.* The science dealing with matter and energy: *studied physics and chemistry.* **physical, physically, physician, physicist**

pierce | pîrs | *v.* To make a hole in: *might pierce the tire.* **pierces, pierced, piercing, piercingly**

pigeon | **pĭj′ən** | *n.* Any of the family of birds with a stout body, short legs, and smooth feathers: *a pigeon on the roof.* **pigeons**

planet | **plăn′ĭt** | *n.* A celestial body that moves in an orbit but does not produce light by itself: *saw the planet through the telescope.* **planets, planetary, planetarium**

plaster | **plăs′tər** | *n.* A mix of water, lime, and sand that becomes hard in order to form a solid surface: *applied plaster to the wall.* **plasters, plastered, plastering, plasterer**

please | plēz | *v.* To satisfy or give pleasure to: *will please the guests.* **displease, displeases, displeased, displeasing, displeasingly, displeasure**

plentiful | **plĕn′tĭ fəl** | *adj.* Relating to something in ample supply; more than enough: *plentiful sunlight for the garden.* [see *plenty*]

plenty | **plĕn′tē** | *n.* An ample amount or number: *received plenty of gifts.* **plentiful, plentifully, plentifulness**

poison | **poi′zən** | *n.* A substance that can cause sickness or death: *poison from the snake bite.* **poisons, poisoned, poisoning, poisonous**

policy | **pŏl′ĭ sē** | *n.* A written agreement about insurance between a company and an individual: *a fire insurance policy.* **policies**

politics | **pŏl′ĭ tĭks** | *n.* The art and science of government: *studied politics and law.* **political, politically, politician**

pollute | pə **lōōt′** | *v.* To make something harmful to living things: *shouldn't pollute the water with chemicals.* **pollutes, polluted, polluting, pollution, pollutant, pollutants, polluter**

pollution | pə **lōō′shən** | *n.* A condition that is harmful to living things: *the pollution in the river.* [see *pollute*]

popular | **pŏp′yə lər** | *adj.* Being liked by a lot of people: *the popular student.* **popularize, popularly, popularity**

popularity | **pŏp′yə lăr′ĭ tē** | *n.* The condition or quality of being liked by a lot of people: *because the politician had great popularity.* [see *popular*]

portion | **pôr′shən** | *n.* One part of a whole: *received my portion of the payment.* **portions, portioned, portioning**

position | pə **zĭsh′ən** | *n.* **1.** A job: *will ask for a position.* **2.** A point of view; opinion: *a popular position.* **positions, positioned, positioning**

possess | pə **zĕs′** | *v.* To own or have: *does possess many skills.* **possesses, possessed, possessing, possession, possessions, possessor, possessive, possessively, possessiveness**

possession | pə **zĕsh′ən** | *n.* Something owned: *a family possession.* [see *possess*]

possibilities | **pŏs′ə bĭl′ĭ tēz** | *n.* Things that could happen: *possibilities for fun.* [see *possible*]

possible | **pŏs′ə bəl** | *adj.* Capable of being or happening: *a possible outcome.* **possibly, possibility, possibilities**

poverty | **pŏv′ər tē** | *n.* The state of being very poor: *a life of poverty and neediness.*

practically | **prăk′tĭk lē** | *adv.* **1.** Very nearly; almost: *practically ruined the surprise.* **2.** In a useful way: *planned practically for the huge crowd.* [see *practice*]

practice | **prăk′tĭs** | *v.* To do again and again for the purpose of learning or mastering: *will practice the routine.* **practices, practiced, practicing, practitioner, practical, practically, practicality, practicable**

prairie | **prâr′ē** | *n.* A grassy area of flat land: *cows grazing on the prairie.* **prairies**

praise | prāz | *v.* To express approval of: *praise your talent.* **praises, praised, praising, praiser**

praising | **prā′zĭng** | *v.* Expressing approval of: *is praising your work.* [see *praise*]

precious | **prĕsh′əs** | *adj.* Valuable; worth a great deal: *precious diamond.* **preciously, preciousness**

prefer | prĭ **fûr′** | *v.* To like more: *would prefer to stay here.* **prefers, preferred, preferring, preference, preferable**

preside | prĭ **zīd′** | *v.* To act as a chairperson: *to preside at the convention.* **presides, presided, presiding, presider, president**

ă pat / ā pay / â care / ä father / ĕ pet / ē be / ĭ pit / ī pie / î fierce / ŏ pot / ō go / ô paw, for / oi oil / ōō book / ōō boot / ou out / ŭ cut / û fur / th the / th thin / hw which / zh vision / ə ago, item, pencil, atom, circus
©1977 by Houghton Mifflin Company. Reprinted by permission from THE AMERICAN HERITAGE SCHOOL DICTIONARY.

press | prĕs | v. To exert force; push: *will press the red button.* **presses, pressed, pressing, pressure, pressures, pressured, pressuring, pressurize**

pressure | prĕsh′ər | n. The force exerted on a unit area of something: *air pressure.* [see *press*]

prevail | prĭ vāl′ | v. To succeed: *will prevail in the contest.* **prevails, prevailed, prevailing, prevailingly, prevailer**

previous | prē′vē əs | adj. Happening or existing before something else: *a previous date.* **previously**

prime | prīm | adj. First in importance or rank: *his prime interest in language.* **primes, primed, priming, primely, primer**

principle | prĭn′sə pəl | n. 1. Standards relating to moral behavior: *a person with a principle.* 2. A law or rule: *a principle of economics.* **principles, principled**

privilege | prĭv′ə lĭj | n. An uncommon right or benefit granted to someone: *received the privilege of speaking first.* **privileges, privileged**

probable | prŏb′ə bəl | adj. Very likely to be true: *the probable reason they are late.* **probably, probability, probabilities**

procedure | prə sē′jər | n. A way of doing something: *careful procedure.* [see *proceed*]

proceed | prə sēd′ | v. To go forward, especially after being interrupted: *will proceed with the exercise program.* **proceeds, proceeded, proceeding, procedure, procedures, procedural**

process | prŏs′ĕs′ | n. A series of steps used to do something: *followed the process for planting the flowers.* **processes, processed, processing, procession, processions, processional**

procession | prə sĕsh′ən | n. A group of persons, cars, etc., moving forward in an orderly fashion: *the funeral procession.* [see *process*]

proclaim | prō klām′ | v. To announce officially: *will proclaim peace.* **proclaims, proclaimed, proclaiming, proclamation**

produce | prə dōōs′ | v. To create or manufacture: *will produce interesting toys.* **produces, produced, producing, product, producer, producible, production, productions, productive, productively, productiveness, productivity**

production | prə dŭk′shən | n. The act of creating, producing, etc.: *production of clothing.* [see *produce*]

profess | prə fĕs′ | v. To pretend; claim to know: *does profess an interest in science.* **professes, professed, professing, professor, professors, profession, professional, professionalism**

professor | prə fĕs′ər | n. A teacher; an instructor: *a lecture by a famous professor.* [see *profess*]

profit | prŏf′ĭt | v. To make money or other gain from business: *will profit from the big sale.* **profits, profited, profiting, profitable, profitably**

profiting | prŏf′ĭt ĭng | v. Bringing about a gain or advantage: *was profiting the shoe store.* adj. Rewarding: *a profiting experience.* [see *profit*]

progress | prŏg′rĕs′ | n. Steady improvement: *made progress in his studies.* — | prə grĕs′ | v. To make steady improvements: *will progress through the course.* **progresses, progressed, progressing, progression, progressive**

prominence | prŏm′ə nəns | n. Importance: *had prominence in the community.* **prominent, prominently**

prominent | prŏm′ə nənt | adj. Well-known: *a prominent man.* [see prominence]

prompt | prŏmpt | adj. Punctual; immediate: *a prompt answer to the letter.* **prompts, prompted, prompting, prompter, promptly, promptness**

propose | prə pōz′ | v. To suggest; put forward for consideration: *propose a policy.* **proposes, proposed, proposing, proposer, proposal**

proposed | prə pōzd | v. Suggested: *proposed a picnic.* [see *propose*]

prosper | prŏs′pər | v. To have success; do well: *if the business will prosper and grow.* **prospers, prospered, prospering, prosperous, prosperously, prosperity**

prosperity | prō spĕr′ĭ tē | n. The condition of being wealthy and successful: *lived in prosperity and health.* [see *prosper*]

prosperous | prŏs′pər əs | adj. Very successful; flourishing: *a prosperous shop.* [see *prosper*]

prune | prōōn | v. To trim branches from a plant to make it grow or look better: *will prune the lilacs.* n. A dried plum: *ate the prune.* **prunes, pruned, pruning, pruner**

public | pŭb′lĭk | n. People as a whole: *for the public.* **publics, publicity, publicize, publish, publisher, publication, publications**

publication | pŭb′lĭ kā′shən | n. Printed matter that is sold: *a news publication.* [see *public*]

pursue | pər **sōō**′ | *v.* To chase after in order to catch: *will pursue the criminal.* **pursues, pursued, pursuing, pursuer, pursuit, pursuance**

puzzle | **pŭz**′əl | *v.* To confuse: *might puzzle the young boy.* **puzzles, puzzled, puzzling, puzzler**

puzzling | **pŭz**′lĭng | *adj.* Perplexing; confusing: *puzzling behavior.* [see *puzzle*]

Q ▆▆▆▆▆▆▆▆▆▆▆▆▆▆▆▆

qualify | **kwŏl**′ə fī′ | *v.* To become eligible for a position, award, job, etc.: *will qualify for the scholarship.* **qualifies, qualified, qualifying, qualifier, qualification**

quality | **kwŏl**′ĭ tē | *n.* Degree of worth; value: *quality of the silk.* **qualities**

quantity | **kwŏn**′tĭ tē | *n.* Amount: *a small quantity of fresh fruit.* **quantities, quantify**

quiet | **kwī**′ĭt | *adj.* 1. Silent; making little noise: *a quiet child.* 2. Calm: *a quiet bay.* **quiets, quieted, quieting, quieter, quietest, quietly, quietness**

quietest | **kwī**′ĭt ĭst | *adj.* 1. Most silent; making the least amount of noise: *the quietest animal.* 2. Calmest: *the quietest lake.* [see *quiet*]

quotation | kwō **tā**′shən | *n.* The act of repeating the exact words of: *quotation of the speech.* **–Quotation marks–**Punctuation used to set off the exact words of a speaker. [see *quote*]

quote | kwōt | *n.* A quotation; the exact words of someone else: *a quote from a poem.* **quotes, quoted, quotable, quoting, quoter, quotation, quotations**

R ▆▆▆▆▆▆▆▆▆▆▆▆▆▆▆▆

rally | **răl**′ē | *n.* A large meeting organized to support a cause: *a rally for the candidate.* **rallies, rallied, rallying**

rather | **răth**′ər | *adv.* 1. Somewhat; more than a little: *rather noisy.* 2. More willingly: *would rather leave.*

real | **rē**′əl | *adj.* Actual; true: *the real reason for the absence.* **really, realize, realization, reality, realities, realism, realist, realistic**

reality | rē **ăl**′ĭ tē | *n.* A real thing or an actual fact: *the reality of the situation.* [see *real*]

receipt | rĭ **sēt**′ | *n.* A written statement that something, such as money or a letter, has been received: *receipt for the bicycle.* [see *receive*]

receive | rĭ **sēv**′ | *v.* To take something that has been offered or sent: *might receive a package.* **receives, received, receiving, receiver, receipt, receipts**

recognize | **rĕk**′əg nīz′ | *v.* To know or be able to identify because of past experience or learning: *can recognize his former teacher.* **recognizes, recognized, recognizing, recognizer, recognizable, recognition**

recommend | rĕk′ə **mĕnd**′ | *v.* To praise or to speak highly to someone about something or someone: *recommend a restaurant.* **recommends, recommended, recommending, recommendation, recommendable**

refer | rĭ **fûr**′ | *v.* To turn to for information: *will refer to the map.* **refers, referred, referring, referral, reference, references, referenced, referencing, referrer**

reference | **rĕf**′ər əns | *n.* A source of information: *a dictionary for reference.* [see *refer*]

refrigerate | rĭ **frĭj**′ə rāt′ | *v.* To keep cool or to make cool: *will refrigerate the juice.* **refrigerates, refrigerated, refrigerating, refrigerator, refrigerators, refrigeration**

refrigerator | rĭ **frĭj**′ə rā′tər | *n.* A machine, usually boxlike, that keeps foods at a low temperature: *fruit in the refrigerator.* [see *refrigerate*]

regain | rĭ **gān**′ | *v.* To get back again: *will regain authority.* **regains, regained, regaining**

register | **rĕj**′ĭ stər | *v.* To sign up for something, such as classes, contests, etc.: *will register for Art II. n.* A book for an official list of names, items, etc.: *signed the register at the wedding.* **registers, registered, registering, registration, registry, registrar**

regret | rĭ **grĕt**′ | *n.* A feeling of sorrow for wrongdoing: *regret for his actions. v.* To feel sad or sorry about: *will regret my mistake.* **regrets, regretted, regretting, regrettable, regretful**

regretting | rĭ **grĕt**′ĭng | *v.* Feeling sorry about: *regretting the decision.* [see *regret*]

reign | rān | *v.* To rule: *will reign for 50 years. n.* A period of power for a ruler: *the king's reign.* **reigns, reigned, reigning**

ă pat / ā pay / â care / ä father / ĕ pet / ē be / ĭ pit / ī pie / î fierce / ŏ pot / ō go / ô paw, for / oi oil / ŏŏ book / ōō boot / ou out / ŭ cut / û fur / *th* the / th thin / hw which / zh vision / ə ago, item, pencil, atom, circus
©1977 by Houghton Mifflin Company. Reprinted by permission from THE AMERICAN HERITAGE SCHOOL DICTIONARY.

relief | rĭ **lēf′** | *n.* The removal or decreasing of pain, distress, or anxiety: *got relief from the headache.* [see *relieve*]

relieve | rĭ **lēv′** | *v.* To make easier or to reduce the pain of: *will relieve the pain.* **relieves, relieved, relieving, reliever, relief, reliefs**

religion | rĭ **lĭj′ən** | *n.* Any particular organized system of belief: *the religion of the people.* **religions, religious, religiously, religiousness**

remedy | rĕm′ĭ dē | *n.* A cure; something used to ease pain or cure disease: *a remedy for a headache.* **remedies, remedied, remedying**

remember | rĭ **mĕm′bər** | *v.* To recall to mind or think of again: *remember the good times.* **remembers, remembered, remembering, remembrance**

remembrance | rĭ **mĕm′brəns** | *n.* **1.** A memory of a person, thing, or event: *my remembrance of her.* **2.** A memento or souvenir: *a remembrance to place on the mantle.* [see *remember*]

render | rĕn′dər | *v.* To cause to become: *to render helpless.* **renders, rendered, rendering, rendition**

repeat | rĭ **pēt′** | *v.* To do or make again: *will repeat the experiment.* **repeats, repeated, repeating, repeatedly, repeater**

repeatedly | rĭ **pē′tĭd lē** | *adv.* Again and again: *to hit the ball repeatedly.* [see *repeat*]

represent | rĕp′rĭ **zĕnt′** | *v.* To serve as the delegate or agent for: *represent the voters.* **represents, represented, representing, representation, representable, representative**

representative | rĕp′rĭ **zĕn′tə tĭv** | *n.* One qualified to serve as an official agent: *a government representative.* [see *represent*]

request | rĭ **kwĕst′** | *n.* The act of asking for someone or something: *a request for more help.* *v.* To ask for: *will request a new seat.* **requests, requested, requesting**

require | rĭ **kwīr′** | *v.* To need; demand: *will require tools.* **requires, required, requiring, requirement**

resemble | rĭ **zĕm′bəl** | *v.* To be like; look like: *might resemble my sister.* **resembles, resembled, resembling, resemblance**

reserve | rĭ **zûrv′** | *v.* To order in advance or hold for a specific time or date: *will reserve a table.* **reserves, reserved, reserving, reservedly, reservation**

reside | rĭ **zīd′** | *v.* To live; make one's home: *will reside in a brick house.* **resides, resided, residing, resident, residential, residence, residences, residency**

residence | rĕz′ĭ dəns | *n.* A place where a person lives: *moved to another residence.* [see *reside*]

resides | rĭ **zīdz′** | *v.* Lives in a place for an extended period; makes one's home: *resides in the apartment next door.* [see *reside*]

resist | rĭ **zĭst′** | *v.* To oppose; work against: *can resist an attack.* **resists, resisted, resisting, resistant, resistance, resister**

resistance | rĭ **zĭs′təns** | *n.* The act or capability of opposing: *resistance to the weather.* [see *resist*]

restaurant | rĕs′tər ənt | *n.* A building, room, etc., where the public can purchase meals: *ate at a Chinese restaurant.* **restaurants**

revolt | rĭ **vōlt′** | *n.* A rebellious act against authority: *a revolt in the country.* **revolts, revolted, revolting, revolution, revolutionary, revolutionist, revolutionize**

roam | rōm | *v.* To wander about: *to roam through the woods.* **roams, roamed, roaming, roamer**

robot | rō′bət | *n.* A humanlike machine that does routine work at command: *a robot that cooks and cleans.* **robots**

rural | rŏŏr′əl | *adj.* Of the country: *a rural environment.* **rurally**

S

salary | săl′ə rē | *n.* A fixed amount of money paid for regular work: *saved part of her salary.* **salaries, salaried**

sanitary | săn′ĭ tĕr′ē | *adj.* Free from germs; clean: *a sanitary bandage.* **sanitarily, sanitize, sanitation**

satellite | săt′ l īt′ | *n.* A moon or man-made object orbiting a celestial body: *a satellite orbiting Earth.* **satellites**

satisfactory | săt′ĭs făk′tə rē | *adj.* **1.** Pleasing: *a satisfactory meal.* **2.** Enough to meet the demands or needs: *satisfactory supplies.* [see *satisfy*]

satisfy | săt′ĭs fī′ | *v.* To put an end to a desire or need; fulfill: *will satisfy my hunger.* **satisfies, satisfied, satisfying, satisfyingly, satisfactory, satisfaction**

sauce | sôs | *n.* A preparation, often liquid, used to improve the taste of food: *mustard sauce.* **sauces, sauced, saucing, saucy, saucer, saucers**

saucer | sô′sər | *n.* A small, shallow dish on which to set a cup: *a china saucer.* [see *sauce*]

scale | skāl | *v.* To climb to the top: *will scale a nearby mountain.* **scales, scaled, scaling, scaly**

scaling | skā′lĭng | *v.* Climbing to the top of: *scaling the ski slope.* [see *scale*]

scent | sĕnt | *n.* **1.** The trail of a distinctive odor left in passing: *if the dog will follow the scent.* **2.** Odor, especially a pleasant one: *scent of perfume.* **scents, scented, scenting**

scheme | skēm | *n.* A plan for accomplishing something: *a scheme for making money.* **schemes, schemed, scheming, schemer**

scholar | skŏl′ər | *n.* A person with much knowledge or intellect: *a literary scholar.* **scholars, scholarly, scholastic, scholarship, scholarships**

scholarship | skŏl′ər shĭp | *n.* A grant of money given to a student to further his or her education: *won a college scholarship.* [see *scholar*]

science | sī′əns | *adj.* Relating to the study of natural events: *a science teacher.* *n.* Knowledge based on observed facts: *theories of science.* **sciences, scientific, scientist, scientists**

scientist | sī′ən tĭst | *n.* A person with knowledge of a branch of science: *a scientist in the biology lab.* [see *science*]

secretary | sĕk′rĭ tĕr′ē | *n.* A person who has been hired to do clerical work, such as typing, filing, etc.: *typing for the secretary.* **secretaries, secretarial**

seize | sēz | *v.* To take possession of by using force; grab: *to seize the equipment.* **seizes, seized, seizing, seizer, seizure**

senate | sĕn′ĭt | *n.* A governing or lawmaking group: *meeting of the senate.* **senates, senator, senators**

senator | sĕn′ə tər | *n.* A member of a governing council: *if the senator voted for the law.* [see *senate*]

sensation | sĕn sā′shən | *n.* Feeling; something perceived by the senses: *sensation of heat.* [see *sense*]

sense | sĕns | *n.* Any of the functions of sight, hearing, smell, taste, and touch: *a fine sense of hearing.* **senses, sensed, sensing, sensory, sensation, sensations, sensational, sensationally, sensible, sensitive**

sentiment | sĕn′tə mənt | *n.* **1.** An opinion: *have the same sentiment about politics.* **2.** A feeling; an emotion, especially a tender one: *the sentiment of joy.* **sentiments, sentimental, sentimentally, sentimentalist**

serve | sûrv | *v.* To work for; to provide goods and services for: *serve the customers.* **serves, served, serving, servant, service**

service | sûr′vĭs | *n.* **1.** Work done for others as an occupation or business: *service necessary to install the automatic washer.* **2.** The armed forces of any country: *joined the service.* [see *serve*]

session | sĕsh′ən | *n.* A meeting of a court, legislature, class, etc.: *a session of Congress.* **—In session**—Meeting. **sessions**

shaft | shăft | *n.* A long, narrow passage: *an air shaft.* **shafts**

sigh | sī | *n.* The act of exhaling while making a weary or sorrowful sound: *a loud sigh.* **sighs, sighed, sighing**

sign | sīn | *v.* To place one's signature on: *will sign the bill.* **signs, signer, signed, signing, signature, signatures**

signature | sĭg′nə chər | *n.* The name of a person, handwritten by the person: *signature on the check.* [see *sign*]

similar | sĭm′ə lər | *adj.* Alike in one or more ways: *similar plans for the vacation.* **similarly, similarity, simile**

sincere | sĭn sîr′ | *adj.* Without any false appearance; true: *a sincere friend.* **sincerely, sincerity, sincerest**

sincerely | sĭn sîr′lē | *adv.* Without any falseness; truly: *sincerely happy.* [see *sincere*]

single | sĭng′gəl | *adj.* Not in the company of others; one: *owns a single pet.* **singles, singled, singling, singly, singular, singularly, singularity**

singular | sĭng′gyə lər | *adj.* Of a word that relates to one person or thing: *singular pronouns.* [see *single*]

situate | sĭch′ōō āt′ | *v.* To place; locate: *will situate myself in a sunny location.* **situates, situated, situating, situation**

ă pat / ā pay / â care / ä father / ĕ pet / ē be / ĭ pit / ī pie / î fierce / ŏ pot / ō go / ô paw, for / oi oil / ōō book / ōō boot / ou out / ŭ cut / û fur / th the / th thin / hw which / zh vision / ə ago, item, pencil, atom, circus
©1977 by Houghton Mifflin Company. Reprinted by permission from THE AMERICAN HERITAGE SCHOOL DICTIONARY.

situated | sĭch′o͞o ā′tĭd | *adj.* Located: *situated near a lake.* *v.* Placed or located: *situated herself in the front row.* [see *situate*]

sketch | skĕch | *n.* A fairly rough and quick drawing or design: *a sketch of the campsite.* *v.* To draw: *will sketch a tree.* **sketches, sketched, sketching, sketcher, sketchy, sketchier, sketchiest, sketchily, sketchiness**

ski | skē | *v.* To move on skis: *will ski down the mountain.* **skis, skied, skiing, skier**

skid | skĭd | *v.* To slide out of control on a slippery surface: *might skid on the icy road.* **skids, skidded, skidding**

skidded | skĭd′əd | *v.* Slid out of control: *skidded off the road.* [see *skid*]

skiing | skē′ ĭng | *v.* Moving on skis: *downhill skiing.* [see *ski*]

sleigh | slā | *adj.* Of a sleigh: *a sleigh driver.* *n.* A cart on runners for use on snow, usually pulled by a horse: *a ride in a sleigh.* **sleighs, sleighed, sleighing**

slumber | slŭm′bər | *n.* Sleep: *restful slumber.* **slumbers, slumbered, slumbering, slumberer**

smother | smŭ*th*′ər | *v.* **1.** To lavish too much emotion on: *may smother with love.* **2.** To cover one food with another: *to smother with mushrooms.* **3.** To suffocate: *could smother in the hot room.* **smothers, smothered, smothering**

sneeze | snēz | *v.* To make air pass suddenly through the nose and mouth by an involuntary spasm: *will sneeze when near flowers.* **sneezes, sneezed, sneezing**

snoop | sno͞op | *v.* To search or to pry secretly: *won't snoop into other people's business.* **snoops, snooped, snooping, snoopy, snooper**

social | sō′shəl | *adj.* Friendly: *a social person.* [see *society*]

society | sə sī′ĭ tē | *n.* **1.** All human beings living together as a group: *today's society.* **2.** A community: *living in a peaceful society.* **social, socials, socially, sociable, sociably, sociableness, societies, socialize, socialism, socialist**

solid | sŏl′ĭd | *adj.* Of definite shape and volume; not liquid or gaseous: *a solid substance.* *n.* A substance with definite shape and volume: *change from a liquid to a solid.* **solids, solidify, solidifies, solidifying, solidity, solidarity**

solution | sə lo͞o′shən | *n.* The answer to a problem: *the solution requires thought.* [see *solve*]

solve | sŏlv | *v.* To find a solution or answer to: *will solve the riddle.* **solves, solved, solving, solvable, solver, solution, solutions**

somersault | sŭm′ər sôlt′ | *n.* A roll in which one turns head over heels: *performed a somersault.* **somersaults**

sorrow | sôr′ō | *n.* Grief; sadness: *felt sorrow at the loss.* **sorrows, sorrowed, sorrowing, sorrowful, sorrowfully, sorrowfulness**

sorrowful | sôr′ə fəl | *adj.* Feeling, causing, or showing grief or sadness: *a sorrowful expression.* [see *sorrow*]

specify | spĕs′ə fī′ | *v.* To state or point out in a precise manner: *must specify a choice.* **specifies, specified, specifying, specifier, specific**

specimen | spĕs′ə mən | *n.* A part of a whole, representing the whole; a sample: *a specimen of saltwater fish.* **specimens**

spell | spĕl | *v.* To name or write the letters forming a word: *can spell my name.* **misspell, misspells, misspelled, misspelling, misspeller**

splash | splăsh | *n.* The sound of splashing, or of making drops of liquid fly about: *the splash from the dive.* **splashes, splashed, splashing, splasher, splashy, splashier, splashiest**

splendor | splĕn′dər | *n.* **1.** Great brightness or brilliant light: *splendor of the sun.* **2.** Magnificent show; glory: *the splendor of victory.* **splendid, splendidly, splendors, splendorous**

startle | stär′tl | *v.* To fill with alarm: *the noise would startle us.* **startles, startled, startling**

stationery | stā′shə nĕr′ē | *n.* Paper and envelopes for writing letters: *stationery with my address.*

subscribe | səb skrīb′ | *v.* To order and agree to pay for a certain number of issues of a newspaper or magazine: *will subscribe to two magazines.* **subscribes, subscribed, subscribing, subscriber, subscription**

substance | sŭb′stəns | *n.* Material or matter: *composed of a soft substance.* **substances, substantial, substantially**

substitute | sŭb′stĭ to͞ot′ | *adj.* Taking the place of someone or something else: *substitute player.* *n.* Someone or something that takes the place of another: *a substitute for sugar.* **substitutes, substituted, substituting, substitution**

succeed | sək sēd′ | *v.* **1.** To achieve something desired or tried: *will succeed in business.* **2.** To come next in line; to follow after: *will succeed the king.* **succeeds, succeeded, succeeding, success, successful, successfully, succession, successor**

successful | sək **sĕs′**fəl | *adj.* Having achieved success, or a favorable result: *a successful investment.* [see *succeed*]

succession | sək **sĕsh′**ən | *n.* The act of following in order or sequence: *appeared in quick succession.* [see *succeed*]

suffice | sə **fīs′** | *v.* To be enough: *if two meals will suffice.* **suffices, sufficed, sufficing, sufficiency, sufficient, sufficiently**

sufficient | sə **fĭsh′**ənt | *adj.* Enough; the amount that is needed: *sufficient money to purchase lunch.* [see *suffice*]

summary | **sŭm′**ə rē | *n.* A condensed version of a larger work, noting all the major points: *a summary of the story.* **summaries, summarize, summarizes, summarized, summarizing**

summon | **sŭm′**ən | *v.* To call for: *will summon the principal.* **summons, summoned, summoning, summoner, summonses**

suppose | sə **pōz′** | *v.* To think possible; assume; expect: *to suppose we can attend.* **supposes, supposed, supposing, supposedly**

surrender | sə **rĕn′**dər | *v.* To give up; give oneself up: *won't surrender to the enemy.* **surrenders, surrendered, surrendering**

sway | swā | *v.* **1.** To bend to one side: *will sway away from the building.* **2.** To swing back and forth or from side to side: *will sway his legs when seated.* **sways, swayed, swaying, swayer**

swaying | **swā′**ĭng | *v.* Bending to one side: *swaying toward the east.* *adj.* Swinging back and forth or from side to side: *swaying trees in the wind.* [see *sway*]

swell | swĕl | *v.* To expand: *can swell from a bruise.* **swells, swelled, swelling, swollen**

swollen | **swō′**lən | *adj.* Expanded; increased in size or volume: *swollen ankle.* [see *swell*]

syllable | **sĭl′**ə bəl | *n.* A single sound that forms part of a word or a whole word: *the stressed syllable.* **syllables, syllabication, syllabicate, syllabic**

sympathy | **sĭm′**pə thē | *n.* A feeling of pity for another's problem: *felt sympathy for his loss.* **sympathies, sympathetic, sympathetically, sympathize, sympathizes, sympathized, sympathizing, sympathizer**

T

tariff | **tăr′**ĭf | *n.* A special tax or duty imposed by a government on imports and exports: *the tariff on wheat.* **tariffs**

temper | **tĕm′**pər | *v.* **1.** To soften or moderate: *will temper the decision with kindness.* **2.** To harden or strengthen a metal by alternately heating and cooling it: *to temper the steel.* **tempers, tempered, tempering, temperate, temperately, temperature, temperatures, temperament, temperamental**

temperate | **tĕm′**pər ĭt | *adj.* Moderate; quite mild: *temperate weather.* [see *temper*]

temperature | **tĕm′**pər ə chər | *n.* The degree of cold or heat: *body temperature.* [see *temper*]

theft | thĕft | *n.* The act of stealing: *the theft of the painting.* [see *thief*]

theory | **thîr′**ē | *n.* Statements that explain something, usually by using logic: *a theory about life on Mars.* **theories, theorize**

thermometer | thər **mŏm′**ĭ tər | *n.* An instrument used to measure temperature: *used a thermometer to check the fever.* **thermometers**

thief | thēf | *n.* A person who steals secretly: *caught the jewel thief.* **thieves, thieved, thieving, thievery, thievish, theft, thefts**

thorough | **thûr′**ō | *adj.* Complete; extremely careful: *a thorough search.* **thoroughly, thoroughness**

though | thō | *conj.* Although; while: *though we waited.* *adv.* However: *though not now.*

tire | tīr | *v.* To make weary or tired: *will tire after the long race.* **tires, tired, tiring, tireless, tirelessly, tiresome, tiredness**

tireless | **tīr′**lĭs | *adj.* **1.** Unceasing: *tireless efforts.* **2.** Not tiring easily: *a tireless gymnast.* [see *tire*]

tongue | tŭng | *n.* The fleshy organ in the mouth, having taste buds: *the scratchy tongue of the kitten.* **tongues**

torment | **tôr′**mĕnt′ | *n.* Intense pain: *the torment of the injury.* **torments, tormented, tormenting, tormentor**

torrid | **tôr′**ĭd | *adj.* Extremely hot and dry: *torrid desert.* **torridly, torridness**

ă pat / ā pay / â care / ä father / ĕ pet / ē be / ĭ pit / ī pie / î fierce / ŏ pot / ō go / ô paw, for / oi oil / ŏŏ book / ōō boot / ou out / ŭ cut / û fur / *th* the / th thin / hw which / zh vision / ə ago, item, pencil, atom, circus

©1977 by Houghton Mifflin Company. Reprinted by permission from THE AMERICAN HERITAGE SCHOOL DICTIONARY.

tough | tŭf | *adj.* **1.** Difficult: *a tough job.* **2.** Able to withstand strain without tearing; having strength: *tough rope.* **tougher, toughest, toughly, toughen, toughness**

trifle | trī'fəl | *n.* A small amount: *a trifle nervous.* **trifles, trifled, trifling**

triumph | trī'əmf | *n.* A victory; success: *the triumph of the team.* **triumphs, triumphed, triumphing, triumphant, triumphantly**

trophy | trō'fē | *n.* A prize received for a victory: *a trophy from the tennis tournament.* **trophies**

U

uncomfortable | ŭn kŭm'fər tə bəl | *adj.* Not comfortable; uneasy: *an uncomfortable meeting.* [see *comfort*]

uncommon | ŭn kŏm'ən | *adj.* Not common; unusual: *uncommon weather for this area.* [see *common*]

unconscious | ŭn kŏn'shəs | *adj.* **1.** Lacking awareness; unable to think: *unconscious after the fall.* **2.** Not aware of one's actions: *an unconscious gesture.* [see *conscious*]

underdog | ŭn'dər dôg' | *n.* The contestant believed least likely to win: *surprising victory of the underdog.* **underdogs**

unexpected | ŭn ĭk spĕk'tĭd | *adj.* Coming without warning: *an unexpected visitor.* [see *expect*]

unfortunate | ŭn fôr'chə nĭt | *adj.* Not having good luck: *unfortunate accident.* [see *fortune*]

unite | yōo nīt' | *v.* **1.** To join together for a common purpose: *will unite the political parties.* **2.** To join together to form a whole: *can unite the two halves.* **unites, united, uniting, unity, unify, unifies, unified, unifying, union**

universe | yōo'nə vûrs' | *n.* All that exists; the whole of reality: *a universe full of people, plants, and animals.* **universes, universal, universally, universalize, university, universities**

university | yōo'nə vûr'sĭ tē | *n.* An institution of higher education: *studied literature at the university.* [see *universe*]

unnecessary | ŭn nĕs'ĭ sĕr'ē | *adj.* Not necessary; not required: *unnecessary amount of noise.* [see *necessary*]

unusual | ŭn yōo'zhōo əl | *adj.* Not usual; extraordinary or rare: *an unusual pet.* [see *usual*]

use | yōoz | *v.* To operate or put into service: *can use the phone.* **misuse, misuses, misused, misusing, misuser, misusage**

usher | ŭsh'ər | *n.* A person who guides people to their seats in a theater, auditorium, etc.: *an usher at the play.* **ushers, ushered, ushering**

usual | yōo'zhōo əl | *adj.* Ordinary; common: *if the usual schedule changes.* **unusual, unusually, unusualness**

utmost | ŭt'mōst' | *n.* The very most that is possible: *the utmost of her abilities.* *adj.* Of the greatest degree or extent: *the utmost peak.* [see *utter*]

utter | ŭt'ər | *adj.* Completely; total: *utter joy during the ceremony.* *v.* To speak: *to utter my name.* **utters, uttered, uttering, utterance, utterer, utterable, utterly, utmost, uttermost**

V

variety | və rī'ĭ tē | *n.* A number of different types, often within a general grouping: *variety of flowers.* [see *vary*]

vary | vâr'ē | *v.* To change; make different: *to vary the design by adding color.* **varies, varied, varying, various, variously, variety, varieties, variable, variation**

vast | văst | *adj.* Great in area or extent: *vast mountain range.* **vaster, vastest, vastly, vastness**

vegetate | vĕj'ĭ tāt | *v.* To grow, sprout, or exist as plants do: *will vegetate in the sunny window.* **vegetates, vegetated, vegetating, vegetation, vegetable, vegetables, vegetarian**

venture | vĕn'chər | *n.* An enterprise or task involving a risk: *because the trip was a venture.* **ventures, ventured, venturing, venturesome, venturer**

vertical | vûr'tĭ kəl | *adj.* Straight up and down: *drew a vertical line.* **vertically, verticalness**

vertically | vûr'tĭ kə lē | *adv.* Relating to a line that runs straight up and down: *vertically even lines.* [see *vertical*]

vessel | vĕs'əl | *n.* A boat or ship, usually quite large: *a sailing vessel.* **vessels**

vicinity | vĭ sĭn'ĭ tē | *n.* A place or region nearby: *in the vicinity of the park.* **vicinities**

victim | vĭk'tĭm | *n.* A person or animal injured or killed: *victim of the hurricane.* **victims, victimize, victimizes, victimized, victimizing**

violent | vī'ə lənt | *adj.* Severe, harsh, or dangerous: *violent tornado.* **violently, violence**

visible | vĭz'ə bəl | *adj.* Able to be seen: *visible stain on the shirt.* **visibly, visibility, visibleness, invisible, invisibly, invisibleness**

vocation | vō kā′shən | *n.* A profession that one is skilled at or has been trained for: *a vocation in the arts.* **vocations, vocational**

voluntary | vŏl′ən těr′ē | *adj.* Done of one's own free will: *voluntary donation to charity.* [see *volunteer*]

volunteer | vŏl′ən tîr′ | *v.* To offer to do something of one's own free will: *will volunteer for the project.* **volunteers, volunteered, volunteering, voluntary, voluntarily**

W

weary | wîr′ē | *adj.* Very tired; exhausted: *felt weary after the trip.* **wearies, wearied, wearying, wearier, weariest, wearily, weariness**

week | wēk | *n.* A time period of seven days: *vacationed for a week.* **weeks, weekly, biweekly**

weird | wîrd | *adj.* Mysterious: *weird noises.* **weirder, weirdest, weirdly, weirdness**

whimper | wĭm′pər | *n.* A low, mournful sound: *a whimper from the puppy.* **whimpers, whimpered, whimpering**

whisper | wĭs′pər | *v.* To speak quite softly and often secretly: *whisper to the librarian.* **whispers, whispered, whispering, whisperer**

whispered | wĭs′pərd | *v.* Spoke quite softly: *whispered a secret.* [see *whisper*]

wither | wĭth′ər | *v.* To dry up; shrivel: *will wither from lack of rain.* **withers, withered, withering**

witness | wĭt′nĭs | *n.* A person who saw something occur; an eyewitness: *a witness to the crime.* **witnesses, witnessed, witnessing**

wrestle | rĕs′əl | *v.* To fight hand to hand, trying to force one's opponent to the ground: *will wrestle with his brother.* **wrestles, wrestled, wrestling, wrestler**

Y

year | yîr | *n.* Twelve months: *spent a year in Europe.* **years, yearly**

yearly | yîr′lē | *adj.* In every year: *a yearly meeting. adv.* Once a year: *visits yearly.* [see *year*]

yield | yēld | *v.* To give in; allow to another: *will yield the right of way.* **yields, yielded, yielding, yieldingly, yielder**

youth | yo̅o̅th | *n.* A young person: *a youth from Finland.* **youths, youthful, youthfully, youthfulness**

ă pat / ā pay / â care / ä father / ĕ pet / ē be / ĭ pit / ī pie / î fierce / ŏ pot / ō go / ô paw, for / oi oil / o̅o̅ book / o̅o̅ boot / ou out / ŭ cut / û fur / *th* the / th thin / hw which / zh vision / ə ago, item, pencil, atom, circus
©1977 by Houghton Mifflin Company. Reprinted by permission from THE AMERICAN HERITAGE SCHOOL DICTIONARY.

Yellow Pages

Proofreading Tips

Finding and correcting the spelling errors in your own writing is an important skill. Try these different ways to check your spelling.

1. Read each word letter by letter, touching every letter with a pencil or pen.

2. Read each word letter by letter, putting a dot under every letter.

3. Have a partner read your work aloud while you check it silently.

4. Read your work out loud to yourself.

5. Read your work backwards, word by word, to yourself.

6. Read through your work. Circle any words that look wrong.

7. Look for words and word parts you often misspell. Double-check their spellings.

8. Check for words that are easy to mix up—*too* instead of *two*, *your* instead of *you're*.

9. Type your work on a computer and use the spell checker. Remember that a spell checker only recognizes that a word is correctly spelled, not that it is correctly used.

10. Find correct spellings wherever you can. Here are some ideas:

    • Try writing the word different ways until it looks right.

    • Say the word slowly. Spell all its syllables.

    • Use what you know about spelling rules, letter sounds, and word shapes.

    • Look for the word on your Personal Spelling List.

    • Have you seen the word somewhere? in a book? on the wall? Find it again.

    • Check the lists in these Yellow Pages.

    • Check a dictionary.

    • Ask someone.

Now make up your own ways to find correct spellings!

Spelling Rules

There are many spelling rules, but only a few of them do most of the work. Nearly all the rules here tell how to add endings to words. *(See pages 190–192 for some of these endings.)* **Unlike some spelling "rules," these work most of the time!**

FORMING PLURALS ("more than one")

Add *s* to most words:
>aprons
>operas
>exhibits

Add *es* to words ending with *s, ss, sh, ch, x*:
>buses
>dresses
>wishes
>patches
>boxes

Change the *f* or *fe* at the end of some words to *v* and add *es*:
>calf, calves
>wolf, wolves
>life, lives
>shelf, shelves
>self, selves
>knife, knives

Know the few nouns that change their spellings:
>child, children
>foot, feet
>mouse, mice
>man, men
>woman, women
>tooth, teeth

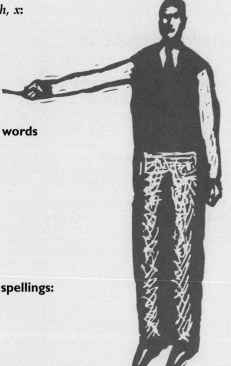

ADDING ENDINGS BEGINNING WITH A VOWEL TO...

...Words Ending with a Vowel Plus a Consonant

Double the final consonant of a one-syllable word:

> bag, bagged
> grip, gripper
> get, getting
> rot, rotten

Double the final consonant of words with more than one syllable when the last syllable is accented:

> permit, permitted
> regret, regretting

Don't double the final consonant when the last syllable is not accented:

> model, modeling
> travel, traveler

ADDING ENDINGS TO...

...Words Ending with Silent E

Drop the final *e* when adding an ending that begins with a vowel:

> hurdle, hurdling
> hostile, hostility
> scrape, scraper
> nerve, nervous

Keep the final *e* when adding an ending that begins with a consonant:

> active, actively
> resource, resourceful
> gentle, gentleness

ADDING ENDINGS TO...

...Words Ending with Y

Add the ending right onto the root when the word ends with a <u>vowel</u> + *y*:

> joy, joyous
> journey, journeyed
> employ, employment
> betray, betraying

Change the *y* to *i* before adding the ending when a word ends with a <u>consonant</u> + *y*:

> lady, ladies
> shiny, shiniest
> lucky, luckily
> try, tried

I BEFORE *E*

Remember the rule:
i before *e*, except after *c*, or when rhyming with *say*, as in *neighbor* and *weigh*:

> believe
> ceiling
> sleigh

but learn the exceptions, too:

> seize
> either
> their
> neither
> weird
> height
> leisure

Spelling Strategies

Perfect spellers are hard to find, but almost anyone can be a good speller. The differences between good spellers and bad spellers are:

> Good spellers know when words are spelled incorrectly. Bad spellers don't.

> Good spellers proofread and correct themselves. Bad spellers don't.

Following are some strategies for improving your spelling. Try them all. Then think of your own.

PERSONAL WORD LISTS

Make lists—or a personal dictionary—of words you use in your writing. Use them as your own personal references.

1. **Difficult Words.** Collect words that are difficult for you to spell. Write them in alphabetical order so they're easy to find. Study them. Write them. Have a partner test you, and use the Proofreading Tips on page 178 to check your spelling. When you can spell and write a word with ease, cross it out and add a new one. Keep changing your list, and don't let it get too long.

2. **Writing Bank.** The best stories you will write are about what you know. Collect the correct spellings of words that name:

   - family, friends, classmates, people you see and do things with

   - places you go, where they are, what they look like, what you do there, where you live

   - things you do, what interests you, what you wish for, your hobbies, your collections

   - sports, movies, video games you enjoy

   The personal words in your Writing Bank can give you ideas for writing.

3. **Personal Computer File.** If you use a computer, dedicate a file to your personal word lists. Be sure to proofread your word list even if you spell check it. *Sum thymes the spell check excepts a word as write, butt its knot the word yew mien two ewes.*

STUDY TIPS

The list of words you can spell easily gets longer as you study and use words from your regular spelling lists and your daily writing. Here are some ways to learn new words for your list.

1. **S-H-A-R-P.** Use the S-H-A-R-P study procedure on page 3 in your spelling book to study spelling words, difficult words, personal words, or any other words you use in your writing.

2. **Hard Spots.** Pay special attention to parts of a word that give you trouble. Study them extra hard. Be on the lookout for these every time you write.

3. **Memory Tricks.** If all else fails, try a memory trick to remember difficult spellings.

   • Make up a spelling-helper pronunciation: princi**pal**, choc-**o**-late.

   • Use meaning-helper word parts: the **real** in **real**ity; the **ear** in h**ear**.

   • Make up your own memory-helper saying. For example,

      A fri**end** is a fri**end** to the **end**.

      There's one *s* in *s*and in the de*s*ert, and two *s*'s in *s*trawberry *s*hortcake for de*ss*ert.

APPROXIMATION

When you are writing a first draft, you sometimes want to use an exact word, a great word, but you haven't yet learned to spell it. Instead of stopping to make sure you get it right the first time, try this:

1. **Spell the word as best you can.** (This is called "approximation." It means "close, but maybe not quite right.")

2. **Circle the word and continue with your writing.**

3. **After you have finished the first draft, go back and correct the circled word.**

Then add the word to your Personal Word List, study it, and use it the next time you are writing.

240 Most Useful Words

If you can spell these words, more than half of what you write will be correctly spelled. (Words marked * are often misspelled.)

A	B	C	D	E	F	G	H	I
*about	back	called	day	eat	family	game	had	if
after	be	came	did	end	father	gave	happy	I'm
*again	bear	can	*didn't	even	fell	get	has	in
all	*because	car	do	ever	find	girl	have	into
also	bed	cat	dog	*every	fire	give	he	is
*always	*been	*come	*don't		*first	go	head	it
am	*before	*could	door		fish	*going	*heard	*its
an	best		down		five	gone	help	*it's
and	big				food	good	her	
another	black				for	got	here	
any	book				form		him	
are	boy				found		his	
around	brother				*four		home	
as	but				*friend		horse	
asked	*by				fun		*house	
at							how	
away								

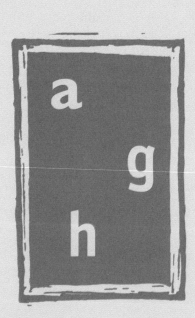

J

just

K

*knew
*know

L

land
last
left
like
*little
live
long
look
*lot
love

M

mad
made
man
*many
may
me
men
money
more
*morning
most
*mother
much
my

N

name
need
never
new
next
nice
*night
no
not
now

O

of
*off
oh
old
on
*once
one
only
or
other
our
out
over

P

*people
place
*play
put

R

ran
*really
red
ride
*right
room
run

S

*said
saw
say
school
see
she
should
sister
small
so
*some
*something
*sometimes
*soon
spring
started
still
*summer
*swimming

T

take
tell
ten
*than
that
the
*their
them
*then
*there
these
*they
thing
think
this
three
*through
time
to
told
*too
took
tree
tried
two

V

*very

W

walk
want
wanted
was
water
way
we
well
went
*were
what
*when
*where
*which
while
*white
who
why
will
with
woods
work
*would

Y

year
yes
you
*your

words

Homonyms and Other Troublesome Words

Some words sound alike but have different spellings and meanings. They are easy to confuse when you write.

accept, except

Please **accept** my invitation.

Everyone was invited **except** me.

allowed, aloud

Smoking is not **allowed**.

The teacher reads **aloud** to the class.

a lot (2 words)

I have **a lot** of homework today.

already, all ready

He's **already** finished.

Now he's **all ready** to leave.

ant, aunt

An **ant** was on my sandwich.

My **aunt** and uncle are here!

ate, eight

Who **ate** the last piece?

We hiked for nearly **eight** hours.

been, bin

Where have you **been**?

She stored the vegetables in a **bin**.

blew, blue

Everyone **blew** whistles at the same time.

I'm black and **blue** from the scrimmage.

by, buy

Come **by** when you're finished.

You can **buy** whatever you want.

capital, capitol

Begin each sentence with a **capital**.

The state **capitol** is a beautiful building.

cent, sent, scent

It didn't cost a **cent**.

Someone **sent** it to her.

The perfume has the **scent** of roses.

chews, choose

He **chews** each bite slowly.

Let's **choose** up teams!

close, clothes

Did you remember to **close** the door?

I have to hang up my **clothes**.

do, dew, due

Do you remember what you did?

The grass was still wet with morning **dew**.

When is our science report **due**?

for, four

I'll buy something **for** you.

I need **four** pencils for school.

hear, here

Did you **hear** a scraping sound?

We're the only ones **here**.

heard, herd

He **heard** the soft lowing of the cattle.

The **herd** was a bit restless.

hole, whole

Put the round peg in the round **hole**.

You have to finish the **whole** puzzle.

hour, our

It'll take at least an **hour**.

We'll do **our** best.

its, it's

The ball has lost **its** bounce.

Maybe **it's** time to get another one.

know, no

Does he **know** her?

I have **no** idea.

knows, nose

Nobody **knows** the way.

His sensitive **nose** will find the way.

lay, lie

Lay the boxes on the floor.

Now go and **lie** down for a while.

lets, let's

Everyone **lets** him do what he wants.

Let's wait and see what happens.

new, knew

Is that a **new** shirt you're wearing?

I **knew**, because it was so smooth.

not, knot

We're **not** going to be able to go yet.

Can you untie this **knot**?

past, passed

It's half **past** nine and I'm finished.

We **passed** the slow-moving truck.

peace, piece

Everyone prefers **peace** to war.

My favorite **piece** is the crusty corner.

plain, plane

He wore a **plain** green sweater.

The **plane** prepared for takeoff.

presents, presence

The **presents** were wrapped in white paper.

Her **presence** in the room quieted the class.

principle, principal

He is a person of high **principles**.

"The **principal** is your pal" is a mnemonic device.

quit, quite, quiet

I wish he'd **quit** talking.

I'm not **quite** ready to go yet.

The baby's sleeping so try to be **quiet**.

right, write

Do we turn left, or **right**?

Why don't you **write** yourself a letter?

some, sum

Don't you have **some** homework?

The **sum** of 3456 + 6543 is 9999.

stationary, stationery

The fort was a **stationary** target.

The letter was written on pink **stationery**.

than, then

No one can run faster **than** you!

She sang one song, **then** she sang another.

there, their, they're

Put it over **there** by the sink.

Are the campers in **their** cabins?

They said **they're** going to help us.

theirs, there's

Are these jackets **theirs** or yours?

Where **there's** smoke, **there's** fire.

through, threw

She walked **through** the gate.

You **threw** away a perfectly good boot!

to, too, two

Go **to** jail.

Go there directly, **too**.

Do not collect **two** hundred dollars.

way, weigh

Show me the **way** to go home.

That must **weigh** a ton!

weak, week

I'm not as **weak** as I look.

In a **week**, they're going on vacation.

wear, where

What are you going to **wear**?

If I knew **where** we're going, I'd tell you.

weather, whether

We're having mild **weather**.

We'll go **whether** it rains or not.

which, witch

I don't know **which** book to read first.

Is she the good **witch** or the bad one?

who's, whose

Who's ready for dessert?

Do you know **whose** hat is on the chair?

wood, would

The ship model is carved from **wood**.

He said he **would** probably sell it.

your, you're

Is this **your** book?

Thanks, **you're** a good friend to return it.

Common Contractions

A contraction is a word made by joining two words. An apostrophe is used to take the place of the letter(s) left out.

is + not = isn't   it + is = it's

Contractions are not difficult to spell once you understand the way they are formed.

VERB + *not*

is	isn't
are	aren't
was	wasn't
were	weren't
have	haven't
has	hasn't
had	hadn't
do	don't
does	doesn't
did	didn't
can	can't
could	couldn't
must	mustn't
will	won't
would	wouldn't
should	shouldn't

PRONOUN + VERB

		am		I'm
		will		I'll
I	+	have	=	I've
		had		I'd
		would		I'd
		are		you're, we're, they're
you		will		you'll, we'll, they'll
we	+	have	=	you've, we've, they've
they		had		you'd, we'd, they'd
		would		you'd, we'd, they'd
		is		he's, she's, it's
he		will		he'll, she'll, it'll
she	+	has	=	he's, she's, it's
it		had		he'd, she'd, it'd
		would		he'd, she'd, it'd

OTHER CONTRACTIONS

In talk, informal writing, and written dialog, contracted words are common. Each word in column 1, for example, can form a contraction with most words in column 2.

1		2		
who		is		_____'s
what		are		_____'re
when		will		_____'ll
where	+	has	=	_____'s
why		have		_____'ve
here		had		_____'d
there		would		_____'d

Roots and Affixes

A root is a word or word part without additions.
You can often add affixes to roots to make new words.
A prefix is an affix at the beginning of a word.
A suffix is an affix at the end of a word.

danger	root word
en**danger**	prefix + **root**
dangerous	**root** + suffix
en**danger**ed	prefix + **root** + suffix
unen**danger**ed	prefix + prefix + **root** + suffix
dangerously	**root** + suffix + suffix

If you know how to spell the root, how to spell common affixes, and the spelling rules for adding suffixes (See pages 179–180)**, you know how to spell thousands and thousands of words.**

Here are some of the extra words you can spell just by adding prefixes and suffixes to the words **person** and **simple**. Notice that adding a suffix sometimes changes the spelling of the root word.

personify	**person**able	**simpl**er	**simpl**ification
personal	**person**age	**simpl**est	un**simpl**ifed
im**person**al	**person**alize	**simpl**y	over**simpl**ification
inter**person**al	de**person**alize	**simpl**ify	**simple**ton
personality	im**person**ation	**simpl**icity	

The Other Word Forms in your spelling lessons and the following lists will help you multiply the number of words you know how to spell.

PREFIXES

Many of your spelling words are root words that can become new words
with new meanings when a prefix is added. Adding a prefix does not usually
change the spelling of the root word. In addition, many English words are made
of prefixes combined with ancient Greek and Latin root words.

	Prefix	Meaning	Examples
how much,	semi-	half, twice	semifinal, semicircle
how many	tri-	three	triangle, tricycle
	kilo-	thousand	kilogram, kilometer
	micro-	very small	microscopic, microfilm
	dec-	ten	decade, decimal
	mono-	one, single	monorail, monologue
	multi-	much, many	multimillionaire, multipurpose
	bi-	two	bicycle, bilingual
where	sub-	under, below	submarine, submerge
	geo-	earth, of the earth	geography, geologist
	by-	near	bypass, bystander
	circum-	round	circumpolar, circumscribe
	in-	into	inhale, inflate
	inter-	between	interrupt, intercom
	trans-	across, elsewhere	transatlantic, transplant
	under-	below	underpass, underground
	tele-	distant	telephone, telescope
	de-	from	decaf, detour
	mid-	middle	midsummer, midday
	en-	cause to be, in	endangered, enclose
	off-	from	off-line, offshore
	extra-	outside	extraterrestrial, extraordinary
	on-	on	onlooker, onshore
not	im-	not	impatient, immobile
	anti-	opposite of, against	antifreeze, antisocial
	ir-	opposite, not	irresponsible, irresistible
	non-	opposite of, not	nonstop, nonfiction
when	pre-	before	preheat, prefix
	fore-	before, in front of	forefather, forecast
	post-	later, after (in time)	postscript, postwar
	pro-	forward	proceed, progress

extent	super-	over, above, greater	superhighway, superhuman
	over-	too much	overcrowd, overcome
	out-	more	outran, outnumber
who	co-	together	co-author, copilot
	auto-	self, by itself	autograph, autobiography
	self-	self	self-respect, self-taught

SUFFIXES

You can make many new words by adding suffixes to the ends of root words.
The Other Word Forms of your spelling lessons show the many new words
you can spell simply by adding a few endings to the spelling words.

Remember that the spelling of the root word may change when you add a
suffix: **marry/marri**age, **excel/excell**ent, **nerve/nerv**ous. (See the Spelling Rules
on page 180.)

Suffix	Meaning	Examples
-able	able to be	enjoyable, favorable, comfortable, acceptable
-ade	action of	blockade, escapade, barricade, promenade
-age	action of	postage, marriage, package, pilgrimage
-al	relating to	natural, musical, maternal, trial
-ance	state of	allegiance, annoyance, repentance, resistance
-ation	state of	starvation, fascination, inspiration, admiration
-ence	state of being	confidence, dependence, difference, absence
-ent	being or condition	excellent, confident, president, provident
-er	one who, more	teacher, printer, buyer; smaller, larger, faster
-ese	language, native of	Japanese, Chinese, Vietnamese, Portuguese
-hood	state of	childhood, adulthood, falsehood, statehood
-ian	relating to	barbarian, librarian, Houstonian, physician
-ible	causing, able to be	contemptible, terrible, gullible, eligible
-ic	relating to	aquatic, comic, public, historic, lunatic
-ify	to make	simplify, clarify, beautify, mummify, purify
-ing	material that	bedding, frosting, roofing, stuffing, lining
-ion	state of	admission, action, suspicion, companion
-ism	action or condition	enthusiasm, patriotism, baptism, heroism
-ist	one who	dentist, geologist, physicist, aerialist, cyclist
-ity	state of	ability, activity, electricity, locality, vanity
-ive	tending to	adhesive, active, evasive, captive, creative
-ize	to make or do	monopolize, specialize, vaporize, magnetize
-less	without	needless, careless, useless, regardless

-logy	subject of study	mineralogy, biology, phrenology, astrology
-ly	quality of	motherly, hourly, boldly, patiently, dryly
-ment	quality of	agreement, amusement, argument, amazement
-ness	state of	kindness, happiness, quickness, firmness
-or	action or work	governor, inventor, escalator, doctor, actor
-ous	nature of	mountainous, envious, ambitious, generous
-ship	state of	friendship, statesmanship, hardship, ownership
-some	action or state	awesome, tiresome, quarrelsome, burdensome
-teen	number 10	thirteen, fifteen, seventeen, nineteen
-th	number	fourth, tenth, hundredth, thousandth, millionth
-ty	state or condition	priority, loyalty, honesty, unity, conformity
-ure	action	failure, censure, exposure, enclosure, signature

CREDITS

Cover Design: Design Five

Photography: Joseph Sachs

Text Illustrations:
Lamberto Alvarez
    pages 25, 41, 72, 78, 109, 129, 146
Shana Greger
    pages 37, 63, 99, 125, 147
Jennifer Hewitson
    pages 17, 74, 82, 122, 123
Claude Martinot
    pages 7, 10, 106, 107, 139
Jennifer D. Paley
    pages 9, 13, 49
Lauren Scheuer
    pages 81, 89, 110, 113, 114, 134
Brad Teare
    pages 31, 69